PENNY BURKE & JOA

From Granny Panties to Thongs

The Mourning After

To my mom and best friend - Sheila
Dad was the wind beneath your wings...
you are mine.
Your personal journey is what inspired this book.
I love you – P

To my three beautiful daughters Erica, Danielle, and Elise.
You are the best part of every day.
I love you – J

We do not grow up planning for life as a widow, or the isolation that we'll feel after losing our life companion, friend, and lover. Most of us grow up prepping for fairytale lives stocked with immortal health, and eternal love. We day dream of raising children, spoiling grandchildren, and traveling after we retire. Then, without warning, and without a back-up plan, John Lennon said it best, "Life is what happens to you while you're busy making other plans."

The whole is greater than the sum of its parts...

Debbi Pace - Penny's sister-in-law and friend. We both thank you for your brilliant design efforts. The book cover and page layouts are exactly what we wanted. You are an extraordinarily talented woman.

Cynthia Savitt - You make granny panties look great! Thank you for being our model for the book cover and for your life-saving proofreading.

Aileen Burke - Penny's adventurous mother-in-law who allowed us to test shoot the cover with her. Thank you for going above and beyond!

John Sanderson - A talented photographer. Thank you for generously donating your time and bringing the cover of our book to life.

Jeff Tobe - We met you at Panera, for bagels and coffee. We left with a world of knowledge.

Pam - A.K.A. cupid – Our thoughtful and loving friend, who is also the woman that introduced us! It was on that "fateful" girl's night out that Joanie and Penny met for the first time.

Joanie's enthusiasts:

My Parents - Dad, you were warm, wise, and wonderful. I miss you very much. Mom, you are a wonderful person who always puts a smile in my day. Thank you for giving us a "test-run" and pre-reading all of the stories. Although some of them were painful for you, many made you laugh out loud. What inspired me most of all was when you said that each and every one of them made you feel good...because they were so relatable.

Elise - My daughter and Penny's adopted daughter. You meticulously read each story, and made editorial corrections that were well-founded. We're happy to see that college is paying off! We know that we tested your patience, and you never lost your cool. Lastly, thank you for allowing us to take over the dining room table, impeding on your right to watch television in your own home.

Danielle and Erica - My daughters. Danielle, thank you for rushing home from Zumba class when I called you in a panic…because I had accidentally erased the entire book from my computer. In less than a minute, you found the files and were headed back to the gym. You never made fun of me, at least not to my face. You are my hero. Erica, throughout this whole adventure you helped me maintain my sanity, and made me laugh when I needed it the most. You are a remarkable young woman, who is wise beyond her years.

Rhonda - My beautiful sister - You are a confidante, friend, and my eternal cheerleader.

Geoff, Jessica, Alex, Ada, Stan, Marybeth, Barb, Jayna, Pat, Nieves, Mary Ann Eisenreich and Penny - My "unconditional" group of supporters and friends. All of you bring so much joy to my life. I am blessed to know each and every one of you.

Sweet Peggy - My lifesaver! Thank you for the endless reams of paper that I went through using your copy machine at all hours of the day and night. Such a good friend…you even made deliveries! Nothing is ever too much for you to do.

Steve - Always my friend. Thank you for all of your editorial inspiration!

Kevin Barrett - You are a great photographer, and a very patient man. I was a little bit bossy while you were doing my photo shoot for the back cover. You are a sweetheart.

Lisa Gordon - You were a launch pad for me, and I thank you for having faith in my writing abilities. I credit you for landing me my first paid assignment! As they say, the rest is history.

Penny's enthusiasts:

Mitch - My husband and best friend. Thank you for your endless encouragement and tireless grammar edits. How lucky I am to have you in my life. I love you 555.

Melissa and Debbie - My amazing sisters. More than anyone, you have both been a significant part of mom's journey and the reason for this book. Thank you for all of your support. I love you both very much and wish that we lived closer.

Mel - You not only changed my mom's life, but you've brightened many others. We share a special bond, and my children are lucky to be able to call you grandpa. I love you.

Margie and Jayne - Your friendship, love, and encouragement mean the world to me.

Lisa - A wonderful sister-in-law. You push me to follow my dreams and always answer my texts no matter what time it is!

Zack and Max - My two beautiful boys. You are my world and I am proud to be your mom.

Introduction

Penny

I never thought that this day would come. The idea for "From Granny Panties to Thongs" was born almost fifteen years ago, when my father passed away. It changed the lives of my sister's and me, but it paled in comparison to what our mom was going through. It had left an enormous void in her life, but fortunately it was not a permanent one. Mom left the safety of her nest and began to spread her wings. At first she attended support groups, and then she began to date. Luckily, I lived nearby and was able to see mom often. It felt great to be able to give her back just a small fraction of what she'd given to me through the years. We talked about dad, and we talked about moving on. Mom loved being married. She acknowledged wanting to leave the door open to finding love again. My role was clear. I wanted mom to know that I supported her no matter what. She had to feel comfortable sharing her innermost thoughts with me, and she couldn't feel that I was judging her.

Initially mom flew low, but she soon began to soar. Navigating this new world was challenging and somewhat scary. We bonded over new topics of conversation, and laughed as mom lamented she had no "dating clothes". We shopped together, and mom's spirit slowly returned. Her story has a happy ending. She fell in love with a wonderful man, and I officiated their ceremony. My family has come to love him, and we are glad they have each other to share their lives with. We still talk about dad, and every year on his birthday we all eat his favorite donut. I've learned, throughout this journey, that the heart has an enormous capacity to love, and that the new love of one doesn't cancel out the love of another. Mom's favorite saying is "most women are lucky to have found true love once in their lifetime, but I am fortunate to have found it twice."

I purchased some books for mom on grieving and loss. They were helpful to her, in the beginning, but she was looking for more than I could give her. She longed to hear "stories" from other widows. I was reassuring, but I hadn't walked in her shoes, and she wanted to hear from other women who had. Had a book such as this been in print at the time, it would have been a vital resource for her. Mom's journey inspired me, and I promised her that I would write this book and dedicate it to her. Somewhere between a full time job and motherhood, my idea for this book fell by the wayside. Sadly, as time passed, it went from the front seat - to the back seat - and ultimately into the back of my minivan. It wasn't until I met my remarkable friend Joanie, almost two years ago, that pen was finally put to paper. She held my feet to the fire and kept us organized and productive. We live in different states, so this was often challenging. Joanie finally said goodbye to her less than sophisticated cell phone and got an I-phone. Working at our computers, for hours at a time, we would converse with one another on I-Chat. We agreed, we disagreed, we laughed our heads off, and sometimes there were tears. At the end of the day, this book was a true labor of love.

Joanie

The first time I met Penny was six months after my dad passed away. My mother was adjusting to her new life as a widow, and I was adjusting to life without a father. My dad was an amazing man, whose mere presence made my world feel safe. He was light in a dark room, a good laugh when nothing seemed funny, and wisdom when something didn't make sense. Penny and I took an instant liking to one-another and struck up a fast friendship. Although our circumstances differed, we had the world in common. The most stand-out difference between us would become the key link that unified us. She had lost her father 15 years earlier, and after only six months, I was still a novice. Penny's mom was happily remarried, while mine was just beginning to venture from her cocoon.

My parents had been married for over 50 years, and as much as I loved my father, I was open to anything (or anyone) new that might present itself in my mother's life. I had witnessed too many scenarios where sons and daughters felt entitled to regulate their surviving parent's recovery process. In an attempt to preserve their own memories, they restricted access to their living parent. The subject of dating wasn't addressed. I understood that my own actions and words could greatly impact my mother's decisions. If she chose to seek male companionship or a spouse again, I did not want to impede her in any way. Quite the contrary, I wanted to be a part of it. If she chose not to, then that was perfectly fine too.

Penny learned that I was a writer, and shared her decade-long idea with me. When she told me the proposed title...From Granny Panties to Thongs, I told her to count me in. Having been involved in writing, most of my life, I believe it was either fate or our fathers that brought us together. I had been thinking about publishing my first novel, and was in the process of weighing my options. After meeting Penny, I knew this was the book I wanted to write. That night, over a glass of wine, we joined forces and decided to write this book together.

The Women

We've had the unique opportunity to speak with some remarkable women who had been widowed. Their reasons for wanting to participate varied, but they shared one common denominator; they all wanted to reach out, and inspire. Through the pages of this book, they wanted to communicate with you and let you know you're not alone. These women represent a wide range of ages, backgrounds, and circumstances. In spite of their differences, we found that they were very much the same. When they crossed over the threshold to find love again, they felt like beginners. Meeting the opposite sex brought them the same worries that they had experienced in their teens.

Their names and some of the minor details have been changed, out of respect to privacy. We consciously used exact words, and phrases to preserve the integrity of each story. Many told us that they had never shared these personal details with anyone before, not even their own children. There were tears as they relived some of the difficult times in their lives, but there was a lot of laughter and blushing faces too. Each possessed a sturdiness that was both admirable, and enviable.

We thank them for opening up their private worlds and granting us entrance inside.

The Stories

Look Beyond 23

The Beautiful Side to Tragedy 37

Cinderella 49

From Granny Panties to Thongs 63

The 3-Date Rule 67

I'm Doing the Best I Can 79

Getting Under the Sheets 89

Reflections from a Daughter 95

I Met Mine Online 105

There is Always a New Passage 119

Men are Like Buses 129

Destiny 135

Milk, Margarine, and Men 147

I was at Peace 159

*What follows next is honest,
passionate and extraordinarily moving.*

Look Beyond...

*I have come to learn that the tremendous love I feel
for my second husband does not annul the love for my first.
I've learned that new experiences won't erase the memories of old ones.
I've learned that it's okay to miss my late husband when I see
or hear something that carries me back in time. It is not
a measure of the amount of love that I feel in my
second marriage. I believe my first husband gave me
the thumbs up to get married again. Maybe his soul got together
with the soul of my new husband's late wife,
and somehow, the two of them put us together.*

I was married to a man who made me feel I could walk on water. He was the well-grounded type while I was more spontaneous and up in the air. He used to call me his free spirit because, as an artist, I was always so care-free. The two of us worked beautifully together, and although we argued, we never attacked one another. We were married for 30 years, and every year it seemed to get better. One day, he went out to play tennis. He kissed me good-bye and said, "Okay Sophie, I'll see you later." Well, later never happened. He was 66, and I was 58 the day he left me. He died suddenly and without warning. I got a phone call from the hospital, and they asked if I had anybody with me. Right then and there, I knew he was gone. I went to the hospital, and when they confirmed what I already knew, I fainted. They asked if I wanted to see him. I said, "No, he's not here anymore."

After the funeral, I returned home. I felt profoundly alone and almost immediately spiraled into a catatonic state. Remarkably, I have little recollection of those days. I must have simply gone through the motions of my daily routine, and I can tell you that I was afraid of everything. I had emotionally shut down and went into a depression.

I stopped doing my art and stopped teaching. It was so strange because I didn't even want people asking me questions. Their questions seemed so senseless to me. When someone would ask me how I was, I used to want to say: "How the f--- do you think I am?" If they had just let me be and say they were sorry, I think I could have dealt with that. But they wanted to go into my heart, and I wasn't giving anyone an entrance.

Although I have a great support system of friends, I never had children, and my family lives far away. I always thought that people who had children and grandkids milling around them were in much better shape than me. A widowed friend of mine with three grown sons gave me a reality check. She laughed when she told me that her one son who lives in England assured her that he was there if she needed him. Her other two sons had wives and kids of their own, and although they called often, they were busy with their own hectic worlds. She had thought that her nest of children might be enough for her. She shook her head as she told me that it just doesn't work that way: "Sophie, you are very much by yourself." Once that reality set in, I became depressed and went on medication. But, I went on the medication because I wanted to move forward. I looked around and thought, I want a life again; I don't want to just survive.

Another dear friend of mine gave it to me straight: "He's dead, honey, and it's a reality you have to face. He didn't just pass away, he is never coming back." After six months, the clouds parted a little bit, and the severe grief began to evaporate. I forced myself to quit saying no to every invitation, and I started going to dinner with anyone who would ask … men, women, friends, acquaintances, former students, anyone. My rule was, as long as you weren't a rapist, homeless, or into child porn, I would go to dinner with you. At that time, I was trying to change up my sedentary and dull routine. I was also attending a lecture series. One particular lecture that I attended was about how to deal with deep depression. I had walked in feeling upbeat, and as I sat there listening to this well-known speaker talk about the darkness of depression, I had an epiphany. I thought to myself, why do I have to sit and listen to this? Why on earth would I want to learn more about depression when I knew enough already. At the intermission, I got up and left.

About eight months after my husband died, I got a call from a friend who had someone she wanted to fix me up with. I knew who the man was and asked her if this was some kind of joke. He wore gold chains and had a perm! It was totally out of the question. I said to her, "You knew my husband, and you can't be serious." I was ready to get out there again, but I did have some criteria. I wasn't exactly a dog. I wasn't going to go out just for the sake of going out, and I was just as content to stay home and read a book or enjoy an evening with friends.

I didn't actually know how to meet men. This was back in the nineties before there was on-line dating, and I wasn't about to hit the bars, so my best resource was word of mouth. It was about a year after my husband died when I put out an all-points bulletin; I wanted to have a life again and even hoped that one day I'd remarry. The announcement fell flat, and no one called me.

On my own, I thought of a man that I wanted to meet. He was widowed around the same time as me, and by all accounts was supposed to be a nice person who had been a good husband. It was a friend of a friend sort of thing, so I made a phone call to someone who knew him to put the feelers out. She responded with a quick "no," stating that he'd been married 40 years, and wasn't ready. Now, even more determined to meet him, I called someone who knew the man's sister. Again, I was told "no," and that he just couldn't be ready yet. Out of courtesy, they agreed to pass along the message.

It so happened he was ready and called me a few days later. I remember thinking that it was his friends and family who didn't seem to be ready. He sounded pleasant on the phone, and we made arrangements to have dinner. I let him pick me up, and he was very personable but also seemed a little nervous. During dinner, he was telling corny jokes, and all I kept thinking was, "Please God, just get me through the evening." He just kept telling dumb jokes, and it was getting on my nerves. I did think he was sweet though, and I could see that the poor guy was trying. I was old enough and wise enough to appreciate that you can't know the nature of a man from one or two dates. A week later, he called me for a second date. He was a quality guy, not to mention that I heard another woman was after him, so I accepted.

He wanted to take me for Chinese food and to see a movie that had just come out. It's a good thing that I don't embarrass easily because we went to see the movie *Basic Instinct.* He was much more relaxed this time and fortunately had stopped with the corny jokes. The evening felt more authentic, and I began to see a calm and sensitive man. Although I wasn't head-over-heels for him, I wanted to see him again. On the contrary, he was head over heels for me and admitted (later) that he had flipped the moment we met. After *Basic Instinct*, we drove back to my place, and I invited him up for coffee.

When we walked in, he tried to sit down, and I stopped him dead in his tracks. I wasn't exactly diplomatic and burst out, "Don't sit in that chair because it was my husband's favorite!" He stood up and said, "I'm very sorry, and I do hope that he's not sitting there now." We both cracked up. He hugged me as he was leaving, and this time I decided to initiate the next date. "If you aren't doing anything for New Year's, I'll take you to the theater if you take me to dinner." He seemed receptive, but then I didn't hear from him. I was sure that my forwardness had blown it, but he called a week later and was excited for our date. I questioned why I hadn't heard from him, and he said it was because we had already made our plans. He also admitted that he didn't want to scare me off with the rush act. I'm convinced that no matter how much we mature, the interplay and misconceptions between men and women remain the same.

Our third date was pivotal. At the theater, we ran into lots of people that knew me, and he thought I was popular. It was just a fun evening, and afterwards I invited him up for coffee again. We were sitting on the sofa, and he said, "Sophie, you aren't going to send me home now, are you?" We started to get cozy on the couch (in those days we called it necking), and both of us started to get turned on. I guess you could say I broke the mood when I blurted out, "Nothing's going to happen here because of the AIDS thing!" It didn't occur to me that since neither one of us had slept with anyone besides our spouses, this wasn't an issue. I guess it was just a knee-jerk reaction because, at that time, everyone was talking about that.

We gradually talked less and less about our late spouses and our marriages. We talked more and more about ourselves and got to know each other as separate people. We learned each other's likes, dislikes, and idiosyncrasies. After spending decades with the same man or woman, couples can get lost in the comfort of their shared routines. Getting familiar with a new man meant that I would need to be accepting of a new routine. At the same time he was getting to know me, I was also getting to know myself. Without planning it, our relationship began to evolve.

He flew down to Florida to spend a few weeks at his condo, but he only lasted a day before calling me to come join him. He missed me and offered to fly me down. At this point, I had relaxed about the AIDS thing and knew that once I went, we would be intimate. I was really falling hard for this guy, and it was all very exciting to me. I packed my bag with new lingerie and nightgowns and then decided that I would take one more step to look my very best. I wanted to get collagen in my upper lip before going to see him. Well, as luck would have it, I got a whopping, black bruise across my lip from the injection. It was nasty looking, and I was too humiliated to tell him what I had done to myself. So, I smeared white paste over it because it was the only thing that I could find to cover up the black. I didn't know whether to laugh or cry. Oh, this is lovely Sophie, I thought, as I looked at the clown in the mirror. Hopefully he would be too busy looking at my new lingerie to notice my bruise.

When I got off the plane, he was staring at my lip. Not knowing what else to say, he politely asked if something had happened to me. "Yes, I banged into a door." There was no way that I was going to confess that I went for collagen! He drove me and my mustache back to his condo. Once we were inside, his actions suggested that it didn't seem to bother him. We had really missed one another, and within minutes we made love. I felt overjoyed and didn't want the afternoon to end.

This man thought I was top-drawer, and he restored something in me that I didn't imagine could ever bubble up again. As our relationship evolved, I could see that much like my late husband, he was going to love me unconditionally. He made everything easy, and he also happened to be a good lover. We proceeded on an intimate level, and once back home we began seeing a lot of each other. Slowly, his things started showing up at my place, and my things at his. Eight months into the relationship I let him know that I wanted to get married again; that I didn't want to be grandpa's girlfriend. Four months later, we were married.

Our first date (for me) had been a complete wipeout, and I'm thankful that I overlooked his corny jokes and allowed him to be human. The two most inspirational words that I would say to any woman looking for love again would be to "look beyond." Look beyond a little pot belly or a balding head; look beyond a corny joke or a silly remark; look beyond too tall or too short. Just look beyond the shallow things that may seem imperfect. There are a lot of nice men out there, but you can't go looking with a magnifying glass. Instead, take time to peel off some layers and look a little deeper. Look for sensitivity, integrity, compassion and above all, kindness. If you find those qualities, then you've got it all.

Mourning after update: *Sophie has been re-married for 18 wonderful years. She still looks at the sky and talks to her first husband. Sophie no longer gets collagen, and her husband still thinks she banged into a door.*

OUR BRAINS ARE SUDDENLY CONSUMED

WITH HOW DESIRABLE WE WILL BE

TO THE OPPOSITE SEX,

AND WE PRAY THEY WON'T NOTICE

OUR PHYSICAL IMPERFECTIONS.

WE FLOOD THE GYMS, STOCK UP

ON RAZORS, SHOVE WHITENING STRIPS

IN OUR MOUTHS, ANALYZE OUR

WARDROBE IN DISGUST, AND BEGIN

HURLING OUR ONCE FAVORITE

UNDERGARMENTS INTO THE TRASH CAN.

WE ARE THROWN BACK TO THE DAYS OF

INEXPERIENCED ADOLESCENCE.

The Beautiful Side to Tragedy

*The books say not to make any major changes
in the first year after loss, and I believe that's a fair guideline.
People have to do some healing
before they can be successful in a new relationship.
I also think that there is no perfect science to this…
the formula changes with each individual and set of
circumstances. A woman is her own best guide
in deciding how long to wait.*

Looking back, I don't know how I survived the whole thing, but I did. Not only did I get myself through it, but I also got my children through it. For reasons only known to God, I was forced to take a blind journey that would reach into the depths of my soul and test every inch of my being. This emotional journey would take me across some very rough terrain. Come hell or high water, I had made the decision from day one that I was going to land with both feet on the other side. I was only 44 when I got the phone call that changed my life in one split second. My husband, who had been on a business trip, would never make it back home. The vibrant man that I had been married to for 20 years died suddenly, leaving behind our 11-year-old daughter, our 13-year-old son and me.

Like any other mother, I worried about my children's needs first. Personal grief was overshadowed by my innate need to protect them from the pain of their loss. I was fortunate because, at that time, I worked in a health-care facility and had access to professionals who could help pilot me through everything. They helped me with the appropriate dialogue for children so I would know what to say, and more importantly, what not to say. Initially I was in a mental fog and was barely putting one foot in front of the other while I figured out what to do. I come from a large family who did their best to insulate me with support. Some people turn away from God in a time of unconscionable loss, but I did the opposite. It drew me closer and is what helped sustain me for a very long time.

For starters, I kept my routine simple. I made myself get out of bed every single day and never detoured back after the kids left for school. I kept up with my exercise routine and walked the track with my good girlfriend seven days a week. Our walks were my therapy and a significant part of my healing process. Having a trusted friend who listened without judgment, gave me the physical and emotional exercise to keep inching forward. I continued to play in my tennis league and socialize with family and friends, even when I didn't feel like it. I kept my household upbeat and positive; I didn't want my children to dread coming home after school. My husband wasn't coming back, so I allowed myself to accept the things I couldn't change.

Although several men had asked me out, it was a full year before I accepted an invitation. It wasn't on my radar that I wanted to date or that I needed to date, but one particular day I thought, "What the heck?" I had become friendly with a physician at work who had lost his spouse around the same time that I had lost mine. I thought that having a common thread might make it easier for me to take this giant step. He was lonely and trying to befriend me; when he asked me to dinner I agreed. We went out a couple of times, but I never felt any connection with him. I'm a carefree and fun-loving woman, and he was this serious and very cerebral kind of guy. I also didn't feel any real attraction for him which made it easy for me to say, "I'm just not ready yet." He responded by giving me a big lecture about how I needed to explore that inner part of me. His approach felt cumbersome, and I was relieved to stop seeing him.

I was insecure about my ability to get close with someone again. After all, if I got close to a man then that meant I would be vulnerable to loss again. I needed to move forward because I had two kids watching me. If I fell into a pit of emotional despair, then that wasn't going to do them any good. There were days when I had to be a good actress, and there were days when I called my family to come help with the kids so that I could go somewhere to privately fall apart. My kids have done remarkably well, and I believe it's because they never watched me get stuck.

A couple of years passed, and I began going out with another man that I met at work. It was nice to get out and enjoy male company but things just never took-off. I gave it about two months, but still wasn't feeling a connection and decided to break it off. For the second time, I lost interest in the idea of dating and removed it from the radar screen.

Four months after that, I was getting ready to play in a tennis match at my club. The night before, I attended the tournament dinner and was seated next to a man who caught my attention. I'm not sure if it was his light-hearted personality or his noticeable blue eyes, but we instantly connected and I felt an adrenalin rush. He engaged me in this teasing sort of banter that was tinged with a little sarcasm. It was a door-opener for me, and

I liked him. After dinner we weren't ready to say good-night, so we went outside to hit some tennis balls.

The next day I saw him at the tournament and lit up like a Christmas tree. It was this intense feeling of chemistry, and I was actually stunned with how attracted I felt. Where did this feeling suddenly come from? We made some casual plans to get together, but I could sense that he was keeping the brakes on. During the first few weeks, we interacted in a friendship sort of way, and he made no attempt to kiss me. I later found out that he was at the tail-end of a failing relationship and wanted to end things properly before beginning something new. He didn't want to hurt anyone and I admired him for it. "Good, he's not a cheater." I thought. His wife left him, and they divorced after 20 years of marriage. In many ways our feelings of loss paralleled because both of us thought we'd be married for 60 years. This was a blessing for me because the similarities are what helped me to bond with him.

As our relationship progressed, one great difference emerged. I had a lot of trouble seeing us as a couple, mostly because it was just so unfamiliar to be with someone else. This was unfair to him because he saw us as a couple, yet I wasn't ready to publicly acknowledge it. At the time, I didn't realize that there was a name for what I was experiencing — it was called survivor's guilt. With that said, I knew he was worth the effort of overcoming the internal challenges that I faced.

The one road block that continued to plague me was allowing him to get too close. I was falling in love again, and it felt good. However, I was seriously struggling with the idea of losing him if we got too close. The wounds from the death of my spouse had left a lingering insecurity about mortality. I worried that he might die too.

Little by little, my insecurities are evaporating. When they occasionally resurface he'll say, "I'm feeling the wall, and you need to let it out." He's tuned in and allows me to talk ad nauseam about things. By making me feel comfortable in sharing my fears about loss, I found myself growing closer to him. We communicate on a deeper level than I experienced in my marriage. Maybe it's due to maturity, and maybe it's due to loss; either way it feels good.

Intimacy was another hurdle for me to climb over. I know that this will probably seem prehistoric, but my husband was the only man I ever had sex with. Although I was falling in love for a second time, it took many months before I re-discovered my sexuality. I must admit that my boyfriend was a patient man, and I often asked him why he put up with me. He assured me that I was worth the wait.

When I knew the relationship was for keeps, we slowly acquainted each other with our children. I truly believe that children just want their parents to be happy, and they could see that this man made their mom happy. I didn't hide the relationship from my kids, but for a while I kept much of my personal life separate from the daily life I shared with them. In high school, they became more independent and involved with friends. In turn, I became more involved with him.

My boyfriend and I have talked about getting married, but we both agree there's no rush. We each still live in the same house that we shared with our spouse and children. Neither one of us has any desire to begin our new life together in a home with prior personal memories. We agree that it would never feel like our home. Starting a new life together means carrying me over the threshold of a new front door.

There was a time when I thought that I was a weak person, but I know better now. I have come a long way in the last few years, and I attribute that to not plunging in before I felt ready to swim. For me, ready meant waiting until the time felt right, and the time felt right when the man felt right. After my husband had died, both my body and brain shut down. There was a good deal of soul searching that I had to go through, and I had to take baby steps. Finding someone I could trust was what opened the door to starting over again. I do love having a partner and a best friend to share my life with. We're told that we light up a room when we're together, and I never thought I could feel this kind of joy in a relationship again. It is a gift.

There can be a beautiful side to tragedy once you allow yourself to focus on the positive. I find the positive in every day and knew from day one that I wasn't going to let tragedy destroy me or my children. It is not to say that I didn't have bad days, but sadness and despair were only allowed to be part of a day and never a whole day. I had to make a choice, and I chose joy. My new mission is to support other women who have lost someone and to help them see a bright future. I now know that there is light on the other side, but you can't get to the other side until you start the journey.

Mourning after update: *They have been together for two-and-a-half years. Her children adore him and look forward to their wedding.*

ALWAYS YOUNG AT HEART,

WOMEN HAVE A NATURAL NEED TO

LOOK FEMININE AND PRETTY,

WHILE MEN WANT TO BE PERCEIVED

AS STRONG AND VIRILE.

AS THE SAYING GOES,

"LOOK GOOD, FEEL GOOD."

COUPLES WHO HAVE BEEN TOGETHER

FOR YEARS MAY FALL INTO A ROUTINE

THAT PUTS COMFORT BEFORE STYLE.

SECOND-TIME DATERS SEARCH THROUGH

THEIR WARDROBES, ONLY TO FIND

THAT THEY SUDDENLY

"HAVE NOTHING TO WEAR."

Cinderella

Please know that I have once walked in your shoes.
I've felt the same hollowness, the same fears,
the same longing for my old life.
You will mourn the loss of your spouse and feel as if things
will never return to normal again.
You will also wake up one day and know
that it's time to resurface and get on with your life.
When that day comes, be ready
because you just may meet your own prince charming.

My husband and I had been married for half of a century when he died three years ago. He was a strong and educated man who I loved deeply, and sadly he suffered with a lengthy illness during the last few years of his life. It was hard to watch him lose his independence and hard to accept the fact that we had become more like one-and-a-half people than a traditional couple. Days stretched into weeks, months, and then years. Before I knew it, the familiar fibers of my old life were replaced with caretaking. Although I wouldn't have changed a single minute, it was often lonely for me.

After my husband had died, I accepted that I would be living out my remaining years with only memories of a once full life. It's strange to think back on that now because, without planning or preparation, my life has taken a dramatic turn. Three years ago, if a crystal ball had forecasted my falling in love again, I wouldn't have believed it was possible. But it was indeed possible, and I'm living proof. I'm always laughing, full of energy, and enjoying the intoxicating effects of a new romance. I feel like Cinderella, and I'm living a fairy tale. The crazier part of this tale is that my boyfriend tells me every day that he is the lucky one. One last detail ... he is seven years younger than me. I'm still a little uncomfortable saying those words, although I'm not sure why. The age difference is not apparent when you meet us. Years of taking good care of myself have paid off.

Coincidentally, the first time I met my boyfriend was over 35 years ago. He is an attorney and my late husband used him throughout the years for several business ventures. My husband and I were also guests at his wedding. After rummaging through old photo albums, I even found a photo of the four of us together. Having said that, I want to clarify any uncertainties that may be crossing your mind here; this union was NEVER something either one of us had ever thought about or considered. I had always thought of him as "the kid across the table."

When my husband died, I needed to have some legal documents executed, and I didn't know a local attorney to go to for assistance. Some friends gave referrals, but I needed a specialist, so I decided to call him. His office was over an hour commute, but I didn't mind the drive as I still had friends and doctors in the area. Without giving it a second thought, I set up an appointment for later that week.

That morning my son-in-law called me with two tickets to see the dress rehearsal of the opera. The tickets were worth $300, and I hadn't been to the opera for some time, so I really wanted to go. It was a ninety-minute drive from where I lived, so it made sense that I would drive to a friend's house that lived closer. We'd see the opera, and then I could spend the night. Well, neither of my friends could go, so when driving to my appointment with the lawyer, I entertained the thought that maybe we could go together as friends. Why not? We hadn't seen one another since the passing of both of our spouses. We had been friends for many years, and he lived close to the theatre. I decided that if it felt comfortable, then I would ask him to join me.

I arrived a little late to his office, and he was all business. He indicated right away that he only had 20 minutes to meet with me because I was late and he had another appointment that morning. I remember thinking how formal he was (not to mention a little rude), and I could never ask him to go with me. After the document was executed he relaxed a bit, and we caught up on our lives. He talked about his wife's passing several months prior, and it was obvious he was still trying to cope with the loss. I talked about the passing of my husband, and we exchanged some wonderful memories.

We stood up to conclude the meeting, and it just came out of my mouth: "Do you like the opera?" His answer disarmed me. "It's funny you should mention that because I was thinking about going." He slid a paper across his desk with ticket information for the upcoming season. I couldn't help but smile and told him that I had two tickets for the performance that evening and suggested we could go together. He nodded and said he would go. Okay, so that was easy, but I suddenly felt shy and wanted to get out of there. After I left, I kept thinking about the opera ... and the lawyer.

We attended the performance that evening. In fact, we

also went to several others after that. It was surprising how much we had in common, and I was attracted to his intellect and his humor. He was drawn to my passion for life and to the way he felt when in my company. What's interesting to me is that I really didn't know him before. We had only spent time together in the context of attorney-client meetings and at his wedding. After three more operas and a handful of dinners, we were officially dating. Although he was open to discussing our new relationship, I had to initiate the awkward issues. The elephant in the room was, for me, that I was older than my boyfriend and that we had known each other for 35 years in another capacity. We talked about things in an honest and open way while exploring a mine field of issues together. We truly did like each other.

No matter how old we are, the rules of dating are fixed. The same issues that plagued us in our teens are still hanging around. My new boyfriend could go three to four days without calling me. This bothered me immensely so, of course, I brought it up. I told him that I needed the continuity and the connection. He told me that he didn't realize this was an issue and that he wasn't much of a phone person, but he would try harder. Geez, I felt as if we needed a dating manual.

After a few weeks, he asked me to bring my overnight bag. Oh my I thought, this relationship is about to advance to the next level. I was excited but also went into a bit of a panic, worrying about the three things that any other woman would agonize about:

What the heck will I wear?

How can I let him see me naked?

What if he's hoping for things that
I'm not ready for?

I went into my closet and looked at my nightgowns. There were two moo moos hanging in the corner, and both of them were about the same age as me. I shuddered at the thought of slinking out of his bathroom draped in one of these. They weren't going to cut it. I called my close friend, who had traveled down this road, to come shopping with me. She asked me when, and I said "immediately!" We went to Victoria's Secret and I tried on everything from ravish me to take your time with me. I walked out with something feminine that had a subtle hint of suggestion.

I arrived at his home on a Thursday afternoon. We had a glass of wine while chatting by the pool, then later that night went out to dinner. We came back to his house and settled in for the night. The next thing I knew was that the sun was coming up Friday morning. Neither of us had been intimate with anyone in a very long time. In the time that we were dating, intense feelings had developed. We were starting to fall in love, and that night we were like two starving people. We were tired, but sleep wasn't on our agenda.

The next morning I was exhausted, but I felt happy. What I wasn't prepared for was the bizarre reaction of my new boyfriend. His demeanor was detached and almost business-like in the morning. He was polite, but it became clear that he wanted me to go home. His behavior blindsided me, and now I couldn't wait to leave. I was drained, had an hour drive ahead of me, and the man that I had just spent a memorable night with was suddenly a stranger. I felt like a one-night stand and didn't understand what had just happened. There were no tears on the way home, but I felt empty and, quite honestly, I was in shock. Getting home was a blur. I got into bed, took my phone off the hook, and went to sleep.

Several hours later I awoke to my doorbell ringing. My girlfriend was tired of hearing the busy signal on my phone and drove over to hear about my date. I told her that he probably wouldn't be calling me again, and if he did, I wasn't sure I'd go. It seemed that my short-lived fairytale was already over. I had opened myself up and now felt terribly hurt. My friend had a different take on the whole thing. She told me that I would hear from him, and based on her experience, she concluded that he might have freaked out a bit over the unexpected intensity of our night together. This made no sense to me, and I rejected her theory.

Friday night came and went with no call. What a louse, I thought. Then, the call came early Saturday morning. I picked up the phone, still half asleep, and it was him. His voice was serious yet tender, focused yet empathetic. "I am so sorry." he said. He couldn't pinpoint the reason for his freak-out, but I believe that he had felt guilt over the pleasure he had experienced. His wife had been ill for several years, and they had not been intimate for a long time. He had built up an emotional wall throughout his wife's ordeal so he could be strong for her. He never thought about sex or pleasure and unexpectedly, the dam of his emotions had broken during our night together. People are hard-wired differently, and can't always foresee how they'll react to a new situation. Both of us had been married, yet alone, for so long.

He drove up later that morning, and I was overjoyed to see him. We have been together ever since and are both very happy. We aren't sure if marriage is in the picture at this stage of our lives, and I am fine with that. Getting married wouldn't make me feel complete because I'm already there. I have my fairytale ending, and I still feel like Cinderella.

Mourning after update: *Although not engaged, she is sporting a gorgeous diamond band. He is always smiling and remembers to call her every day. They have been together for two years.*

THE DESIRE FOR

INTIMACY AND SEX

IS INGRAINED IN ALL OF US.

OUR LIBIDO LIVES ON.

MANY OF US,

WELL INTO OUR SENIOR YEARS

CAN, AND DO,

HAVE ACTIVE SEX LIVES.

From
Granny
Panties
to Thongs

I grew up with a stylish mom who always wore beautiful, colorful clothes and shoes. Her closet was filled with designer labels, and she got her hair cut at Vidal Sassoon. Quite the contrary ... her underwear drawer looked as if it was from an army barracks. All bras were white, and her undies ranged from white to off-white, covered half her torso and looked more like pillowcases.

It had been 18 months since my dad passed away. Mom had been coming on a regular basis to visit with me and her grandkids, but the visits were precipitously becoming further and further apart. Although my mom was dating, I knew that she hadn't yet found a true love connection. I knew this in part because my mom and I shared her dating secrets, but I also knew because I did her laundry on these weekend jaunts, and her snow-white granny panties were alive and well.

One unforgettable day, I was doing my mom's laundry when something red caught my attention. For a moment, I thought this might be someone else's laundry because clearly this couldn't have been my mother's.

I reached into the washing machine and pulled out a bright red thong! I didn't know whether to feel happy or mortified, but I did know that if my mom was shifting from granny panties to thongs then it meant only one thing ... she was either having sex or thinking about it.

I did the only appropriate thing I could think of in that situation. I went tearing through the house, shouting for my mother while wearing her bright red thong on my head! When I found her, she stood frozen, staring at my head. "Mom, I know this lacy, racy thing doesn't belong to me. So, is there something you want to talk about?" We both burst out laughing, and just like two girlfriends, my mom excitedly began to share the reason why she hadn't been coming around as much. His name was Harold, and the thong was a gift from him.

Mourning after update: *After two years of mating and dating, my mom married her beloved Harold. The granny panties are long gone, and he continues to buy her thongs. They have been together for 14 years.*

The 3-Date Rule

*Though a measured amount
of skepticism is prudent,
we should not judge others too quickly
or too harshly.
To do so
can deny us incredible opportunity.*

After my husband had died, it took me six months to emerge from under the rubble and begin piecing my life back together. It's interesting how our minds work; before his illness, I loved thinking about how long we'd been together. After he had died, I was overcome by how short our time had been. Although the formal term for my new identity was a widow, the reality was that, overnight I had gone from being a *we* to being just a *me*. This new identity didn't come with care instructions, and even though I was surrounded by loving arms, I was very much on my own. I felt like this lump of clay that would have to be shaped and molded into something new.

I joined a support group for widows. Every Tuesday evening, we covered a different stage of grief and were sent home with encouraging words and survival guides. For a while it was helpful, and I enjoyed the close camaraderie. Eventually, I started to feel like I didn't belong there anymore. I wasn't quite sure what I was ready for, but whatever it was, I didn't feel I would find it in the safety of my group. I had been toying with the idea of casual dating and had felt embarrassed to reveal that to them. It was almost a year since my husband died. Some of the women weren't even at the six-month mark. Since no one had approached the topic, I worried about how it would be perceived. In retrospect, I should have opened the door to a healthy discussion on it. I learned later that I wasn't the only one thinking about dating.

Wrapped in the security of titles for decades, it now felt awkward to socialize with married couples. I learned that friends who hadn't lost a spouse just didn't get it. They were unable to grasp the enormity of a loss they hadn't endured. I remember the first time that I ventured from the shelter of my curtain-drawn home to spend an evening with my married girlfriends. I listened as one of them grumbled about a black-tie affair that she and her husband had to attend and watched her roll her eyes about another cocktail dress she would have to buy. She talked about the dull group of professionals that they would be seated with and how she hoped to make an early exit. I remembered going to those boring functions and now felt envious of the safe predictability of her world. At that moment, I became overwhelmed with a sense that we no longer had anything in common.

My other friend saw the teary glaze in my eyes and shifted us from the black-tie conversation. On the drive home, she asked if I would consider going on a date with her husband's old frat brother who was now divorced. They didn't know if I was ready but thought the two of us could be a nice match. The guy's name sounded familiar and, as luck would have it, we both grew up in the same suburb. I told my friend to set things up. He called me, and the following weekend I prepared to go on my first official date.

My date and I were a year apart and had actually gone to the same high school, but our memories of each other were vague. My emotions were all over the place that week as I bounced back and forth between feelings of excitement and wanting to cancel altogether. My daughter stopped over to keep a watchful eye on me while I picked out my outfit for the big night. Her constructive criticism was akin to a firing squad, but we compromised on something simple, youthful, and almost sexy. I then cleared her out of the house and sat down to wait for this complete stranger to pick me up and take me to dinner. Well, not a complete stranger; the adolescent portion of my brain recalled that he had played in our high school band and that his crowd wasn't as cool as mine.

As I peeked through the blinds, my stomach cramped from nerves, sending me to the bathroom. What had I gotten myself into? Suddenly, I was convinced that I wouldn't feel attracted to him or worse yet that he wouldn't find me attractive. I began to obsess. He was a professional, so his post-graduate education eclipsed mine. What if we struggle with conversation and he finds me uninteresting? What if we have nothing to talk about at all? I was sure that other women my age, going on a first date, were far more confident and comfortable.

He pulled into my driveway, and I was already judging him by the color of his car. That was strike one. He smiled as I opened the door and invited him in. In lieu of his good looks, what I noticed first was the piece of chewing gum in his mouth. Although he seemed friendly and polite, I decided that this was another strike against him. I would later learn that he just wanted to have fresh breath. Riding to the restaurant he apologized for the gym bag he had forgotten to take out of his back seat. I could focus on nothing else except for the lingering smell of dirty socks. I added this to his suffering score card. He took me to an Irish pub. As we swapped our mini-bios, he introduced me to tasty new beer and Irish food.

I said goodnight to him at the door with a brief hug before going inside. Then I called my sister who answered after half a ring in anticipation of a detailed report. I told her that he was nice but that I didn't see much point in going out again. In an annoyed voice, she asked, "Did he do something to turn you off?" I conceded that he was a quality guy who was probably worth getting to know, but I just wasn't interested. I waited for her to fire her next round of ammunition. Was he ugly? Did he do something wrong? I explained to her that it wasn't any of those things and that I just didn't think he was my type.

After a moment of silence, my sister offered me some valuable advice. Her single friend uses something she calls the 3-date rule. She laid out the theory about how first dates can feel really awkward because people feel self-conscious about everything, from what they should talk about to whether or not they have food in their teeth. "Knowing you, I'm sure you were judging every little thing about him and picking him apart," she eerily added. Was my sister hiding in the car? She had a good pulse on the evening and had just sized up our entire first date.

Subscribing to her friend's 3-date rule, she encouraged me to get together a second time with my 3-strike man. The theory goes something like this: with comfort levels easing on second dates, people might catch a glimpse of each other's true personality. The third date is insurance to spot any attributes that may have been hiding under the surface. It sounded reasonable, so I agreed to test her 3-date theory if he called.

On our second date, he took me to a fancy restaurant and for the first time, I noticed he had two big dimples when he smiled. Having tossed out my initial check-list, I felt more relaxed and was able to focus on the man sitting across from me. He had a quick wit and an easy way. I wasn't feeling fireworks, but I did feel some sparks. I was grateful for the new perspective that came with my sister's advice. In reality, I wasn't a teenage girl who needed to fall madly in love on the first night. I was a woman with many years of life experience, and that included a thick layer of baggage. This kind man wasn't dissecting me; quite the contrary, he was enjoying the heck out of me. It had been unfair of me to scrutinize him. In reality, his imperfections were no different, or worse, than mine.

I went on a third, fourth and fifth date, at which point I called my sister and presented a new report. "He's sweet, he's bright, he's fun, and I think I might be falling for him." We joked about my initial character assassination, and the trivial things on which I had judged him. I thanked her for allowing me to borrow her friend's 3-date rule. That phone call to my sister was made over four years ago. We are still together and continue to learn new things about each other. My disposable date turned out to be kind, witty, and wise. Looking back, I think that fear was guiding me that first night... I hadn't been on a date in decades. I was ready to sabotage a possible relationship before it even began! Judgment, whether good or bad, should be set aside until someone earns it. Although I have since discovered that my own scorecard is far from perfect, I have also learned that someone's quirks and imperfections can end up being the things we enjoy the most about them.

Mourning after update: *Four years later, she still feels excited every time she sees him. They experience the same ups and downs of any healthy relationship. She has shared the 3-date rule with anyone who will listen.*

IT'S TIME TO KNOCK DOWN

SOME OF THE WALLS

THAT STAND IN THE WAY

WHEN WE'RE READY TO MOVE FORWARD.

WE NEED TO BE ABLE

TO DISCUSS OUR FEELINGS

ABOUT WANTING TO START A NEW LIFE.

MANY OF US WANT TO

MEET A MAN AGAIN BUT ARE SOMETIMES

RELUCTANT TO ADMIT IT.

WHEN A WOMAN GETS DIVORCED,

IT SEEMS THAT EVERYONE

ENCOURAGES HER TO SEEK

A HAPPY RELATIONSHIP AND

TO BE COUPLED AGAIN.

PEOPLE TEND TO

TIP-TOE AROUND WIDOWS.

I'm Doing the Best I Can…

Unless someone has walked in my shoes,
they wouldn't be able to understand the emotional
roller coaster that I've been on. Grieving is a highly
personal journey. The last thing I needed was to be judged
by the very people who were supposed to support me.
My husband's family couldn't comprehend
that I had mourned him before he had died.
Through this adversity, I was able to gain strength.
I hope that each of you will eventually find your own
inner strength too.

My name is Lilly, and my husband Sam died when I was 64 years old. We were married for 27 years, and he was sick for the last nine of them. Prior to meeting Sam, I had a brief marriage that produced two beautiful daughters and then ended in divorce.

Sam had been a life-of-the-party kind of guy. We never had our own children together but had a solid marriage and were good partners and friends. He started to get sick and battled one illness after another, none of which could be cured. High blood pressure, neuropathy, diabetes, lung disease, and several mini-strokes would eventually weaken his once healthy body. Waking up ill every day slowly chipped away at his cheery disposition.

Though it happened gradually, his personality also started to change. He didn't like certain foods anymore and began drinking like a fish. He became depressed and actually retired from his job without telling me. His body was being pummeled with medical challenges, and with that came a complete character change. My once laid-back husband became nasty toward me, often saying that he was miserable and didn't want to be in the relationship anymore. It would have been easy to walk away, but I knew that it was his illness speaking; he was trapped in a cage, of which there was no escape. So, I remained a loyal caretaker. Sam's family didn't witness the emotional outbursts because he could maintain his demeanor for a few hours at a time. When they visited, I cooked dinner for everyone. We went through the motions of a typical family gathering. Our life seemed almost normal to the outside world. His family chose to turn a blind eye to the obvious changes that Sam was facing. As his wife, I was unable to be in denial. My emotional needs and personal grief seemed invisible to them.

Things got pretty rough the last two years as my husband divided his time between nursing homes and intensive care units. I was with Sam every day and ate my meals on the run. I often slept at the hospital and stopped home only to grab a quick shower before work. His prolonged illness resulted in enormous personal debt because his health insurance had exceeded the million dollar limit. We were forced to draw from our savings.

I desperately needed a break and longed to have a leisurely dinner with friends, or to get away for a weekend. I hadn't been out to dinner in almost four years. My husband came from a large family, all of whom loved him dearly, but sadly none of them thought to offer me a reprieve. They would come to visit, but after an hour or two they would retreat to their own predictable worlds. No one offered to stay overnight, but I can't say I blamed them. My husband had open wounds that were not only contagious, but also had to be re-dressed every evening in a sterile field. I longed for a good night's sleep, but we couldn't afford a private nurse as our savings were quickly evaporating. Sam took 48 different medications a day, and I created a spreadsheet to keep track of them all. I was no longer Lilly his wife, and he no longer saw me that way.

In the end, he was in excruciating pain and fell in and out of comas. When he died in my arms it came as an overwhelming relief. All I felt was happiness for him that he no longer suffered. Nobody else seemed to share my feelings, but they hadn't lived through it. I had been worn to the bone with exhaustion and had neglected

myself for longer than I could remember. I had mourned the loss of my husband long before he actually died.
Looking back, I'm amazed at the amount of energy that
I was expending each day. I must have been on auto-
pilot. I'm a believer that in this life, we aren't given more
than we can handle.

After the funeral, his family implied that I did not look
the part of the grieving widow. Maybe this was because
I wasn't weepy or curled up in a ball on my couch. They
met weekly to grieve at Sam's grave and were perplexed
that I didn't want to participate with them in this ritual.
When I did visit the cemetery, I preferred to go alone.
There were many expectations of how I was supposed to
conduct myself, and it was unfair. I was taking the time
to catch my breath and be quiet. More than anything,
I just needed some time to think things through. I was
figuring out how to walk in my own shoes again; to resurface back into the world, solo. I missed my husband
deeply but needed to begin a new life without him.

Sometimes, I would day dream about what it would feel
like to get dressed up and go to a cocktail party or to sit

at an outdoor café and crack open a bottle of wine with friends. I imagined what it might be like to go on a spa weekend or even how it might feel to have male company. Sam's family wanted me to stay at home, every night, and miss my husband. I knew that it was possible to grieve and to move on at the same time.

I attended a support group for widows. It was an open forum where people could commiserate about their losses and talk about the different stages of grief. There was a lot of crying, and I didn't want to cry anymore. In retrospect, I'm not sure what I was hoping to gain from the group. Maybe I was looking for affirmation that it was okay to pick myself up and move on with my life. The support group wasn't supporting the things that I personally needed, so I stopped attending.

My daughters coached me to ignore the opinions of others. "Move forward and keep your eye on the ball. You can't live other people's lives mom, and they can't live yours!" They gave me their endorsement to start socializing and to let go of some of the guilt. It had been six months since the funeral when my 40-year-old daughter said to me, "Mom, guess what, it's time for you to start your life up again." I was a borderline recluse and had been in a state of hibernation for nine years. She reminded me that I was only 64 years young and encouraged me to get out there again. Coming from my daughter, this validation meant the world to me.

One morning, a thought occurred to me. Why not? My daughter was right, I was alive and not getting any younger. Rather than plopping down in front of the television every night, it was time to accept some of the social invitations that I had been turning down. At first it was quiet dinners with friends, and then I got into the swing of things. It felt good to be around healthy and active people, and to get out of the house and hear voices. I enjoyed watching couples interact at other tables, and felt a longing for intimacy when they were affectionate. With my re-entry into the land of the living came a new appreciation for life. Even the simplest things felt enjoyable to me.

A co-worker introduced me to a male friend of hers, and one evening we met for a casual dinner. We were laughing and chatting when as luck would have it, I ran into Sam's siblings at the restaurant. It was awkward beyond belief, but then I didn't know whether to laugh or cry. Their cell phones started flying as they feverishly spread the word to the rest of their family. If it weren't so uncomfortable, the whole scene would have been downright comical. My late husband's family was horrified to learn that I had stepped out to begin socializing again. Later, a couple of Sam's siblings called me in an outrage and expressed their disgust over how I could do this. They intimated that I had behaved in a flaunting and disrespectful manner. It was pretty much a no-win situation for me. The next thing I knew, Sam's family had all un-friended me on their various chat sites. Hallelujah!

Other than an occasional email or phone call, I hear little from my husband's family. Sometimes it's ironic how life unfolds because Sam's sister is now walking in my shoes. Her husband recently suffered a serious stroke, and she is beginning to experience some of the things that I did. Sadly for her, she may soon get it. They were my family for almost 30 years, and they have made it impossible for me to have a quality relationship with any of them.

Although they have suffered their own pain, they never empathized with my pain. Part of me died the day the doctors told me that Sam had only a few more months to live.

Making the choice to move forward was challenging for me in different ways. It meant that I would have to release some of the guilt that I carried. It also meant that some of the people that weren't sympathetic to my needs were going to feel betrayed and hurt. My daughters, although supportive, were sensitive to the idea that one day they might have to share me with someone else. Although my hope was to meet another special man, I never wanted them to worry about my ability to share my heart. I assured them that love multiplies, it doesn't divide.

Mourning after update: *Lilly no longer worries what others will think and follows her own heart. With the help of her daughters, she has posted her profile on an online dating site. There is still no contact with Sam's family.*

Getting
Under
the Sheets

Go for it...

*Afterwards, we lingered
and stayed snuggled up in the contented
warmth of each other's company.
It occurred to me that the sex was minor
compared to the rebirth of
our feeling attractive and desirable again.*

I was the first of my friends to be widowed. It wasn't until after the funeral, when the flood of well-wishers started to thin out, that I realized the enormity of what lie ahead. Although I had a college degree, I had been a stay-at-home mom while my kids were growing up and hadn't worked in years. My husband took care of everything which, in my circle of friends, was the norm. That seemed like a luxury at the time, but now that he was gone, it was an added layer to the growing stack of things I needed to learn. It didn't take me long to master bill-paying, car inspections, investment inquiries, and tax returns. It actually amazed me to see what I could learn to do when I had to ... and I had to. Taking charge of my life felt liberating, and I liked not having to depend on others. It helped relieve my mind of the feelings of loss and it helped me develop skills that would allow for personal freedom.

It was 18 months after my husband died when I asked friends if they knew of any decent men to set me up with. I was lonely and no longer wanted to be the extra seat at dinner tables. I wasn't too keen on the notion of online dating, although I knew of a few success stories from it. My computer skills were elementary (I knew how to email), so the whole concept of it was intimidating. I wasn't in the working world and didn't go to bars, which meant that there wasn't much hope for a chance meeting with someone new. The idea of being fixed up seemed like the most practical approach, and it also didn't scare the living daylights out of me. At first, no one knew of anyone, but then I got a phone call. My friend's husband worked with a guy who was now divorced. They thought we might make a good match and said the guy was up for meeting me. With my consent, he set things up. I guess you could say that I had beginner's luck because it was my first official date with a man, and I didn't feel as if I needed to look any further. Wow, this was easier than I thought it would be. We really hit it off and started seeing each other on a regular basis.

About a month into it, this new romance was showing potential. I was flabbergasted to learn that I could feel as dizzy over a guy as I did in my twenties. I must admit, I was shamefully making excuses to my family so that I could (guiltlessly) gallivant on the weekends with my new boyfriend. It felt like someone had awakened me from the dead and doused my body with adrenaline. We were trying out new restaurants, lingering over coffee, and becoming accustomed to a bartender's last call. When burgers at McDonalds took over two hours, we joked that they named the Happy Meal after us. We were enjoying the heck out of each other.

With the sexual vibes between us starting to go airborne, I reverted back to the rule-book of my youth for guidance. I decided to wait awhile before getting under the sheets with him because premature sex could be the kiss of death in any new relationship.

Sometime during week four, and after enjoying a glass of red wine in my living room, I decided to toss the rulebook out of the window. He felt great, he made me feel great, and I was hungry. After some lusty kissing on the couch, a little voice in my head whispered, "Go for it." Without any resistance from him, I took his hand and led us upstairs. Although we had many years of combined sexual experience, it was a shy moment for both of us. The last time I had been intimate was with my spouse, and the same was true for him.

We had spent the past month learning about each other's lives, but tonight we would be two strangers starting from square one. There was an awkward moment or two, but the maturity that follows us into our middle-age years has also taught us how to laugh at ourselves. Somewhere between a bra unsnapping and a belt unbuckling, I said to him, "Nothing fancy tonight, let's keep it simple." I'm sure he was relieved that I wasn't anticipating bedroom acrobats or for him to perform everything he'd ever learned over the last few decades.

There was a first-time innocence that hovered over the room that night. I was thankful that the lights were low, and I didn't have to worry about my fleshy, loose ends or about my not looking like a centerfold. His thighs were the size of tree trunks, and without thinking, I announced that he had the biggest leg I'd ever seen. As we both cracked up at my choice of words, he thanked me and said, "Every guy wants to hear that." Not ready for the night to end, we went downstairs to resume our private dinner party and to pick at our wilting hors d'oeuvres. We never did make it to the main course. I had a ready, willing, and able man next to me and decided to do what any other red-blooded woman would do. I took his hand, led him upstairs, and said, "Let's do it again."

Mourning after update: *Eight years later they are still together. Neither one of them is anxious to get married again. They still enjoy having private dinner parties with wilted hors d'oeuvres.*

Reflections from a Daughter

After two years of an exhausting fight for life, my dad surrendered to the insatiable hunger of cancer. He and my mother had been married for 55 years. My father was a bigger-than-life kind of guy who made our world a safer place. I always used to say that he was lights in a dark room, a good laugh when nothing seemed funny, and encouragement when something felt hopeless. He was warm, wise, and wonderful.

I watched as my mother sorted through a tangle of emotions, only some of which she could comfortably share. We talked easily about how much he was missed, about how quiet the upcoming holidays would seem, about the influx of paperwork that never seemed to slow, and about how inactive her life had suddenly become. One day, as I sat in the quiet of my parents' once pulsating and vibrant home, I stepped out of my own comfort zone and asked my mom a question that would provoke some particularly delicate reflection. I asked her if, underneath her sadness, she was also feeling a sense of relief that dad was gone. She observed me for a moment while carefully collecting her thoughts. My mother was born of the old school and as a rule didn't share these types of feelings. Her relationship with my father belonged to them. Although our family had always been close, I knew them mostly as my parents and not as a couple. My provocative but honest question kindled a liberating and ongoing conversation that continues to this day.

She admitted to feeling a sense of freedom after my dad died. I listened thoughtfully and without judgment, sensing that my mother had much to say. Although I had been an integral part of their support system after he was diagnosed, I was still on the outside looking in. I was able to go home or go out with friends. I was able to read a book, do an activity, or just be me. My mother recounted the torment of the last two years and the toll it had taken on my dad, on her, on them.

After the initial diagnosis, his first year was met with surgery, treatments, and a grand show of optimism. He continued his role as the pillar patriarch and assured everyone that he would "beat this bastard." At first I believed what he said; partly I was trying to be hopeful, but mostly it was easier. It was easier to be naive and not see the inevitable. It was easier not to talk about his fears and to pretend that he still looked the same. It was easier to let my mother, his wife, take on the load.

Hope faded the second year as this despicable disease took the lead, wearing him down and zapping the life out of him. Travel plans were replaced with hospital stays, daily walks were swapped for television, and dining out was traded for obligatory eating in a recliner chair. At 76, my mother stood healthy and strong and lovingly dedicated her days to his needs. Privately, she longed for the man who had been her handsome, robust, and gallant gatekeeper.

As he became anxious and increasingly short-tempered, she confessed that she sometimes felt resentful and even trapped. On particularly exhausting days, she secretly wished that the end was near and then would feel a sense of guilt and selfishness for her thoughts. Her private world became lonely and isolated as the once familiar threads of their marriage were dying along with him.

My dad's death was a pivotal time for both of us as I realized my mom and I didn't share the same losses. Hers stretched over a much wider terrain than mine. While I had been his daughter, she had been his wife, lover, friend, companion, and confidante. Putting my own needs aside, I became a trusted friend that day, giving my mother silent permission to unleash a mixed bag of grief, guilt, and even her desire for a new beginning.

One of the first of many new beginnings came eight months after my dad died. I had come over for our usual Sunday morning breakfast. My mother, who had never used a computer in her life, began speaking about things that were of a foreign tongue to her. "Some of my friends use something on their computers called Google, and I think I'd like to learn how to do that. They say that you can check out all kinds of things about someone on Google." She then asked me if it was possible to find out where people live if they're in a different state. My mother admitted that she had been feeling curious about a guy from her youth. It was her first teenage love, who she had dumped after she met my father. I knew the name well; my mother had remarked more than a few times over the years what a handsome guy he had been. "He looked just like Cary Grant," she would brag to us.

In my heart, I knew that even if we were able to locate her teenage sweetheart, the odds were against any sort of a reunion. It was more likely that he was either happily married or possibly deceased. All of that seemed irrelevant because more importantly, she was making room for new possibilities in her life. My mother had to start somewhere, and I suppose there was a feeling of safety in the familiarity of an old romance. I didn't question her expectations, because even if nothing materialized from our search, I knew it was healthy for her to think along these lines.

After breakfast, I retrieved my parents' laptop ... the one that my mother didn't know how to turn on. I began by teaching her the bare basics, and even this was no easy feat. After some trial and error, she was able to do a Google search. My mother was quite pleased with her new skills, and I knew that learning the computer would open up a whole new world for her. We began our search, and it took only a few clicks to find the guy. The little bit of information that my mother could remember matched up with a man who was now living 2,000 miles away. Next, we took a shot in the dark to find out if he had a profile online so that we might see if he still had a glimmer of his Cary Grant looks. I continued to instruct her. "Click here mom ... Don't be afraid of the computer ... Now click over there!" And then we both let out a scream. He did indeed have a profile, and we were just one click away from seeing the man that she knew only in her very distant memory.

We both took a deep breath, and with the touch of her finger, there he was. I watched my mother's eyes squint as she struggled to find something familiar in the face of this sweet looking man ... a man who had posted pictures of his wife, children, and many grandchildren. She turned to me and said, "That's not him, it can't be him." But, it was indeed him; he had listed his hometown, high school, college, and career path.

In her mind, he had been frozen in time. In her mind,

he was still the young and handsome guy that she had felt a small yearning to reconnect with. He no longer bared a resemblance to Cary Grant, but the handful of photographs portrayed a happy man. After a few moments, she recovered from her initial shock, and we both sat back and smiled in silence. There was no need for words. This small step back in time was a graceful leap onto a new path that was moving forward.

Mourning after update: *Through one of her searches, my mom found another long lost friend who was now a widower. She contacted him, and they became reacquainted. Although just friends, they occasionally get together for lunch or a movie. She no longer requires my assistance and is able to research anything, or anyone, at lightning speed. My mom has become the family's "Google Queen."*

SOME PEOPLE LOSE A SPOUSE
WITHOUT WARNING, WHILE OTHERS
ENDURE LONG-TERM ILLNESSES
THAT RAVAGE THEIR PARTNER'S BODY
AND SPIRIT, LEAVING BEHIND
A MERE SHADOW OF
WHO THEY ONCE WERE.
LYING IN BED NEXT TO A MAN
WHO IS A GLIMPSE OF
THE HUSBAND SHE ONCE KNEW,
CAN BE PROFOUNDLY LONELY
AND FRIGHTENING.
THE CARETAKER'S WORLD
IS OFTEN ISOLATING AND SEXLESS.

I
Met Mine
...Online

*My best friend and co-workers have commented,
"We finally have her back."
I'm laughing, living, and full of energy again.
I've given myself permission to move forward
and just be me. I was a wonderfully devoted wife
who had a strong marriage
and loved her husband. After he died my life felt hopeless,
but now I can allow myself to dream of a future.*

Now widowed, I found myself thinking about dating. It wasn't enjoyable being the fifth wheel at dinner parties, and I didn't want to spend the rest of my life alone. It had been a year since my husband had passed and I felt ready to trade in my TV remote for a social life. The problem was that I had no idea how to meet men, let alone how to date them. It would have been easier if I had a confidant that understood what I was going through, but I didn't. All of my friends were married, and I wasn't comfortable having this conversation with any of them. Maybe they would have been supportive of my desire to date, but I didn't want to take that chance. My volunteer dating coach was someone I knew well: it was my grown son.

One morning, I took a good long look in the mirror. Of course, we look at ourselves each day, but this time it felt different. I no longer recognized the woman that stared back at me. Was it really me? I wondered when I started to look so worn out. When had I allowed myself to look frumpy, and when had I stopped trying. It had been a long time since I paid attention to my hairstyle, my makeup, or my clothing. Having gray hair hadn't bothered me in years; I grew to accept it. Suddenly, I couldn't stand the sight of it. I assessed this dowdy stranger in the mirror, from head to toe, and knew that it was time to make some changes. Men tend to be highly visual, and I was no vision! I needed a complete makeover if I ever wanted to be asked out on a date.

The first thing that I did was say goodbye to the granny-gray, and colored my hair sunshine blonde. I wasn't done there. Next, it was time to break out of my prehistoric makeup routine and actually learn how to use the stuff. I went to a department store, and one of the girls worked her magic on me. I left with a suitcase of cosmetics, and smiled as I caught my reflection in the mirror.

In another act of emancipation, I cleared my drawers of waist-high grandma underwear and harness bras. For the first time in my life, I went to check out Victoria's Secret. I filled the dressing room with a sampling of every style in the store, and jumped right in. At first, I felt self-conscious about trying on such revealing lingerie. I wasn't sure it would look right on my mature body. I noticed that some of the customers were women like me and realized that feeling sexy was more a state of mind than anything else. It was about feeling feminine and not about looking like a perfect 10. As the cashier rang up my array of lingerie, I looked up at her and said, "Yes, they are all for me!" I left the store that day feeling triumphant.

My son, the dating coach, suggested that I try online dating. I'd be able to converse with the opposite sex without meeting them ... unless I wanted to. It was a good way for me to get back in the saddle from the safety of my own home. I had mixed feelings about signing up for a dating site, but the premise sure beat the heck out of getting picked up at a bar. At first I found this type of dating awkward, but I pushed myself to give it a chance. I would pour a glass of wine and go online! Before long, the online dating sites became my new (and fantastically fun) past-time. I registered on Match.com and E-Harmony, two well-known sites, and stumbled upon "Our Time," another site geared for people in their middle years. I became a regular on all three of them. My coach cheered me on and called me daily for an update. That was refreshing, because there were still people who thought it was too soon to have traded in my gray hair and box of tissues.

Other than the initial investment of time, the profile formats were easy to fill out and were actually a lot of fun. I liked having to dig deep and compile a personality profile. It became a journey of self-discovery. They asked me to answer many questions regarding political views, education, family status, religion, activities, foods, etc. Some of the questions got a bit more personal, but nothing too daunting. The end result was a mini-biography. Although they use all of this information to formulate potential matches, your real identity is kept anonymous. Only the members are allowed to give out their information to potential suitors. So far, so good, I could handle this!

A profile on one of the sites caught my attention, and I decided to message the gentleman. He was a retired state trooper, and he was eight years younger than me … things were about to get interesting. Being that my husband had been a cop, it gave me a feeling of connection, so I sent a cute short message. I read and re-read my message a dozen times before getting up the courage to send it. I went to work, but found myself thinking about the message all afternoon. The end of the day couldn't come soon enough; I couldn't wait to get home! Who was this woman that sprinted home, threw her purse on the sofa, and tore open her computer? I couldn't believe my eyes; not one, not two, but three different men had sent me messages. I skipped over the first two and went directly to the message from the younger trooper. He told me that he liked my profile, and was interested in meeting me. I grabbed the phone to call my son and was so excited that I couldn't get the words out fast enough. We both laughed, as he joked that his mother was officially going to be a cougar.

Two days later, I went to meet my younger man at a local restaurant. My nerves were shot, and my heart was beating. This experience made me realize that, although some things change, other things stay the same. I felt the same angst now as I did when I was 16. Whether we like it or not, there's vulnerability when we meet someone of the opposite sex. It took me a long time to get ready for my date. I wore something feminine that showed off my curves, and although he wouldn't see my new lingerie, I put it on to boost my self-esteem. When he walked into the restaurant, the first thing he said to me was, "Your pictures don't do you justice; you are beautiful." Goodbye, insecurity! I joked and asked him if he liked older women. He said that he hadn't even looked at my age and the only things he noticed were my eyes and my smile. It had been a long time since a man had said things like that to me, and I was just taking it all in. This was definitely going to be fun. We enjoyed the evening and went out a few more times.

Another man had also been showing interest and sending me messages. Although I was not madly in love with my younger guy, I did like him and could date only one man at a time. Out of courtesy, I sent the new guy the following response: "I have recently met a special guy on Match and I'm going to see how the relationship plays out and where it leads. I would be happy to have a pen pal relationship with you, but I'm removing my profile today since I'm dating someone." I went on to wish him good luck in his search, and even gave him my personal email address so that we could be pen-pal friends if he wanted to.

In one month's time, I had polished myself up, was dating a terrific guy, and now I had just offered another man the consolation prize of being my pen pal! He appreciated my honesty and said he'd be happy to correspond with me and offer dating advice if solicited. We struck up a friendship through emailing ... lots of emailing. I found myself looking forward to checking my email, and eventually, I gave my pen pal my phone number. After a month, we decided that we would go out as friends.

The night we met happened to be his birthday. When I arrived at the restaurant, I looked across the crowded room, and our eyes locked. I'm not sure how or why, but that night we both found what we were looking for. Everything seemed to click; we were the same age, shared the same interests and had similar histories. Sparks flew between us, as we closed the place down that night. The next day, my pen-pal removed his profile from the dating site, and I called my younger man to tell him to put his profile back on.

It took some adjustments to feel comfortable in the relationship because everything was new to me. Going blonde and putting on pretty lingerie was easy, but swinging open the door to my sexuality was a different story. Because of my husband's illness, I hadn't had sex in many years. I often wondered if intimacy would find a place in my life again. The younger man and I had kissed and shown affection toward each other, but nothing more than that. We had only been going out for a month and hadn't reached that point. Looking back, the reality was that I just didn't have strong enough feelings for him.

It was quite a different story when I met my pen pal. From day one, we became inseparable and couldn't get enough of one another. It was inevitable that our passionate fondling and kissing was going to have to find a bigger outlet. Within a few short weeks, sex was knocking at our door. Pen pal had been divorced for some time and had dated a fair amount. I worried that he'd find me an inexperienced or unexciting lover. I had been with only one man for my entire adult life.

I didn't know ahead of time which night that things were going to happen. When that night came, I felt self-conscious and insecure. My mind was racing all over the place. I wondered what he'd think of my body, my new under-garments, and most importantly, what he would think of me. I went into the bathroom for a couple of last minute primps and a final glance in the mirror. My heart was pounding through my chest, but I was ready. He lightened the mood, and calmed me down, by telling me how lovely I looked and how good it felt to be with me. He laughed as he patted his own belly, saying that he could stand to lose a few. We made love that night, and it was perfect.

I don't want to make this new relationship sound too easy because along with all of the good, there are also challenges. You have to integrate two different lifestyles, personalities, and habits. Initially, I was more comfortable when we were alone. I've always been private, and I had to get used to his desire to hold my hand in public. He is also more experimental than I am in the bedroom. With that being said, as we grow increasingly more comfortable with one another, I become less shy and more adventurous. He is a mover and a shaker; he likes to travel and dine out frequently. With my husband having been ill for several years, this has been a complete lifestyle change, but I love it.

I decided to wait a couple of months before introducing him to the friends that my husband and I had socialized with. When I did, some gave him a warm reception, while others were cautious and even seemed envious of our explosive new romance. We have been together for about a year and have already traveled extensively. Who would have thought that going on a dating site, in my nightgown, would give me a chance at living again.

Mourning after update: *They are currently planning a three-week cruise. Victoria's Secret has a loyal new customer and she now feels comfortable modeling her lingerie. They are tossing around the idea of living together.*

WHEN A WOMAN MEETS
THAT SPECIAL MAN,
SHE FINDS HERSELF BUYING LINGERIE
AS SHE BEGINS TO EMBRACE HER
RESURRECTED FEELINGS OF SEXUALITY.
THIS IS AN EXCITING TIME,
BUT THE EVOLUTION
FROM GRANNY PANTIES TO THONGS
CAN ALSO BE STRESSFUL.
AS THE MIRROR REFLECTS
A MORE MATURE BODY IMAGE, THE WOMAN
NEEDS TO REMEMBER THAT IT'S
ALL ABOUT HOW SHE FEELS AND THAT
SEXY OR FEMININE UNDERGARMENTS
ARE A MERE HOOD ORNAMENT
FOR THE SEXUALITY WITHIN HER.

There is Always a New Passage…

*It is both painful and therapeutic
to recount the staggering losses that I have
endured in my life. I am telling my story
because I want women to know
that, after loss, they will recover.
They need to give themselves permission
to find a new passage.*

The first part of my story isn't anything extraordinary. My name is Sara. I married my high school sweetheart, and we settled into an old-fashioned and traditional marriage. Life was good, and before I knew it our kids were grown, and we had been married for 38 years. My husband was a healthy man who exercised regularly and was in terrific shape. One August, I could see that he was losing weight, so we made an appointment with a doctor. He was diagnosed with cancer, and twelve weeks later he was gone. It was like I blinked my eyes and my life was yanked out from under me. Everything was being hurled at me so fast that I couldn't process it. It felt like I was playing dodgeball with my hands tied behind my back. I suddenly didn't care about living and no longer knew who I was. So much of it is a blur, but I remember that I would lie on my bedroom carpet and listen to Rachmaninoff. That was 15 years ago. I'm 75 now and have come a long way since then.

Financially, I had no choice but to find a way to make a living. This was probably a gift in disguise because it got me out of the house and kept me physically and mentally busy. I loved the art world and learned to work as a scout. It was a mental challenge to find art that would match the style and taste of people's homes. I was good at my job, it was social, and it meant daily opportunities to meeting people. Men would ask me out, and occasionally I would go, but I didn't like it. It seemed to be more of an effort than fun.

It was about 18 months after my husband died, when a client approached me about this terrific guy that she knew in Atlanta. She asked if I would be interested in meeting him. "Sara, I just have this feeling that you two will hit it off." Although I was living in Connecticut at the time, she said that it wouldn't be a problem. This guy loved to travel, and he could afford to do so. My days were full, but my evenings were lonely, so I agreed to meet him. He called, and we talked on the phone for over an hour. We then starting talking every day, and I couldn't wait to get home from work, anticipating the call. The more I talked to him, the more I liked him. It was a slow and easy way to get to know someone, which was probably the best scenario for me.

There was something mystical about him. He loved

yoga, and he was spiritual and comforting. I enjoyed these things about him. He was also a good bit older than me (15 years). Surprisingly, that didn't bother me because I think that's what I needed at the time. He was emotionally available, and financially in a position to make our long-distance relationship work. We dated for four years, the whole time traveling back and forth. I grew to love him in a different capacity than how I had loved my late husband. Though not madly in love, I was very happy.

Married young, my only intimate relationship was with my husband. I wasn't exactly an open-minded free spirit. In the beginning of this new relationship, I was grappling with the idea of being intimate with a new man. It was time for me to step out of the box and weigh some options. Sex could be intimidating and a little forbidding or it could just be pleasurable and fun. As they say, attitude is everything, and I opted for pleasure and fun.

He asked me to marry him, and I said yes. Life became both emotionally and financially easier after we married. We had a beautiful home and were fortunate to share a comfortable lifestyle. He had a vacation home in Arizona, and we were always off somewhere having fun together. A world that had become uncertain to me now felt insulated and safe. He surrounded me with a brick wall of security, and I suppose that's what I loved most about him. There were different ways to love someone, and I was at peace with that.

We had only been married for six months when he complained that he didn't feel well. He was diagnosed with prostate cancer, and his prognosis was grim. To say I was in shock would be an understatement; this was playing out like a bad movie. He quickly became very sick, and I couldn't believe that this was happening all over again. My wonderful husband was gone within a year, but his last months were dedicated to making sure I would be taken care of, without having any worries.

I immersed myself in work and in anything that would fill my hours and my days. The grief was different this time, maybe because it happened so early on, or maybe because I knew from experience that I would survive.

After some time had passed, a young woman at work asked if I might be interested in meeting her father. This sort of caught me off guard, but I felt flattered that she thought enough of me to ask. Her mother had died a year earlier around the same time as my second husband, and she wanted to see her father resurface again. Having been widowed twice, I was an expert on what I needed to do to pick myself back up. As exhausted as I felt, I knew that the best way to combat loneliness and to purge myself of self-pity was to leap back into the real world. I told the young woman that I would be honored to meet her father.

We clearly did like one another, as we have recently celebrated our five-year anniversary. We live together but have no plans to be married. Our commitment is cemented, and we share a loyal and loving relationship. We travel, take care of each other, and although it's less frequent now, we maintain an enjoyable sex life. I'd say we have a healthier relationship than many of our married friends. Some of the things that I had with my first husband can never be replaced; I think of the other things as new and improved. It's not that the second or third time around is better or worse, it's just unquestionably different.

The loss of my first husband had been enormous and fragmented every inch of my emotional being. He had been my soul mate and the love of my life, but I came to learn that I had the ability to love again. Fifteen years ago, it was my son-in-law who assured me there would be another passage in my life. At that time, I was a lump of sadness and unable to absorb his words, but I always remembered what he said. Now, many years later, I have to agree with him. There is more than one person in this world that can make you feel happy. There is more than one way to love someone, and there is more than one way to live as a couple.

Mourning after update: *They have no plans to marry because Sara fears that she will be widowed again. She says that they share a deep love for one another. Sara's family is accepting of Stuart while his children keep her at a safe distance.*

My mother opened up to me
about her desire to date.
In the beginning
it felt peculiar to engage
in this type of dialogue with her,
but it was my time to give back.
She had close friends
and other loving children,
but she had chosen me
to share these feelings with.
My reaction would weigh heavy
on her decision to move ahead.

Men are
Like Buses…
There's a New
One Every
15 Minutes

My name is Sharon, and I lost my husband to an unexpected heart attack when I was just 61 years old. Looking back on this time in my life, I was in a state of shock and couldn't comprehend the magnitude of the loss I had suffered. With no pressing plans, I did as my family suggested and routinely began attending a support group. It was a group mostly made up of women with a few men sprinkled in. Paul was a likeable man who attended these meetings weekly and often sat next to me. His girlfriend had lost her six-year battle with cancer, leaving him exhausted and lonely. I was hardly looking for a relationship, but when we were together, life felt a bit more normal and safe. We bonded over loss and loneliness, and after a few sessions we continued our conversations outside of the group, over coffee and casual dinners. He was a nice companion and we began spending time together.

A few months into our friendship, my daughter invited us to her home for dinner. We were entering unchartered waters… I was going to her house with a man that was not her father, and I didn't want my grandkids to assume that he was going to try and fill their grandpa's shoes. After a few attempts at begging off, my son-in-law called me. He told me that canceling wasn't an option; that it was just going to be a casual dinner. We were welcomed with open arms, and Paul fell head over heels for my grandkids. On the outside, it must have looked as if we were behaving like a traditional couple, but for me this couldn't have been further from the truth. It was simply that when Paul was around, I didn't feel alone. He called each day, brought beautiful cards, and sent me flowers. There were no deep feelings on my end, but he was what I needed at the time.

It was not until my daughter called me the next morning that she began her analysis: "Paul looks so much older than you. He's extremely quiet. He doesn't know how to dress. He seems to care deeply for you. He is nothing like daddy. Does he have money?"

Before we got off the phone, she said something that made me pause. "You know, mom, this man is serious about you." We talked for a long time, and she could hear that I wasn't genuinely happy or content with him. She pointed out that Paul wasn't spontaneous and had no desire to travel. This was in complete contrast to my adventurous ways. Her perceptions were right-on, and I knew that he wasn't going to be good for me long term. As the months passed, Paul was patient and never asked for more than I was ready to give. Life was predictable, uneventful, and I relished the comfort of still being a couple. He had fallen in love, but I didn't feel the same way.

After a year, we booked a cruise to the Caribbean, and when we returned I knew that he wasn't for me. My daughter insisted that I could never fully move on with my life unless I was willing to cut him loose, and then figure out who I was. "Mom, remember that men are like buses; there's a new one every 15 minutes." I appreciated her honesty, but it was Paul that I needed in my life at the time, and I wasn't ready to give him up.

We dated for almost two years. I went to New York to meet his family, and he was already comfortable with mine. We attended weddings, functions, and holidays together; life just seemed easy with him around. It wasn't until he went to New York by himself that I had thoughts about getting off the bus. While sitting by the pool with a friend, an outgoing and handsome man approached us. We all talked for a while before he left to play tennis. Several days later, my girlfriend called to tell me that the guy at the pool wanted to call me. Although Paul was still in my life, I was intrigued by this new man. "Call him and give him my number."

I was hanging out in my apartment with Paul, my daughter and my grandkids when the phone rang. It was him, and I was surrounded and didn't know where to go. I quickly excused myself to the bedroom and went to the most private place I could find … my walk-in closet. It felt as if only five minutes had passed when my daughter flung open the door and threw her hands in the air in disbelief. She mouthed to me that I had been sitting in there for thirty minutes, I was being rude, and she was leaving. Not my proudest motherly moment, I waved her off and stayed on the phone. We made a date, and I found myself on a real high. When I emerged from the closet, my daughter had left, and Paul was still reading a magazine. I'm not even sure he knew I was gone. The rest of the day I gave consider-

PENNY BURKE & JOAN PEARLSTEIN DUNN

able thought to my situation with Paul. He had faith-
fully filled a void in my life, but I wasn't being fair to
either one of us. Somewhere in that closet, I had found
the strength to do what I needed to do. Later that week,
Paul and I had a long talk, and I told him that it was
time for both of us to say goodbye. I didn't want to hurt
him, but I knew that his 15 minutes were up.

Mourning after update: *Paul is still single. Sharon
only went out with the man from the closet three times
before she pulled out the bus schedule. She is now happily married and hasn't taken the bus in nine years.*

Destiny

We had reached that glorious stage of life,
when we could plan trips, enjoy our private time together,
and just be fun grandparents. I was 58 years young
when all of that came to a crashing halt.
My husband died suddenly, after suffering
a massive heart attack while we were away on vacation.
Nothing can prepare a person for that type of loss.
For a long time, I did nothing but exist.
I gave up exercise, socializing, and was unable
to be the same doting grandmother.

With a daughter and other family living in Florida, I decided to sell my home in New York and head south. My husband was locked deep inside my heart and would be with me no matter where I lived. It was an agonizing decision to leave behind a home filled with cherished memories, and to leave my circle of life-long friends, but I needed to make the move. They were sad to see me go, and I'm not sure that anyone truly understood my need for such a complete change. Being a newly anointed widow, I was now on my own and would have to make decisions that were a right fit for me.

I de-cluttered the house and invited my family over for a shopping spree. They were more than willing to take things off my hands. Cabinets were emptied and years of keepsakes, wrapped in paper, were taken to their new homes. That day of nostalgia was loaded with a healthy mix of tears and amusing moments. One of my kids was smarter than the others and went straight to my bedroom closet for the fur coat. She still has it with the caveat that I'm allowed to borrow it during my winter visits. Our home sold quickly, and I took this to be a sign from above. *He* was telling me that it was okay to move on and be happy.

My sister lived in a conveniently located high-rise with a great view of the inter-coastal waterway. I liked the comfort of being near her and got a place of my own in the same building. The view from my apartment was mesmerizing, and sometimes I would just sit outside and reminisce. It was hard to wake up sad in such a beautiful place, and I began to heal.

I was living in a new state, a new apartment, and had a brand new routine. My calendar was starting to show some ink as I explored the area and met new friends. Some of them were widows, but I made a conscious effort to have a little variety and not fall into a rut. Married friends were a bonus. Maybe they'd have a friend who was looking to meet someone fabulous! There was no rush, but I hoped to one day share my life with someone again. I missed having a daily partner, and I missed being in love. I had now been widowed for almost two years and had gone on a few dates, but nobody worth writing a story about.

It would have been perfect if Mr. Wonderful had just knocked on my door and swept me off my feet, but my children kept reminding me that he didn't know where I lived.

I began making phone calls, starting with Les and Judy, who had been our close friends for years. I asked if they knew of anyone to set me up with. Les stepped right up. A colleague of his, Ben, was divorced, and thinking of moving to Florida. I interrogated Les for additional details, but he offered up only that the guy was personable. It would have been nice to have a headshot, and copy of Ben's credit rating, but I trusted my friends and asked them to give the guy my number.

Ben called me a few days later. He was flying down to look at apartments, and asked me to join him for dinner. We decided to try out a hip sushi restaurant near the beach. I was impressed from the start, when Ben said that he would pick me up at 7:00 p.m. Early bird specials were the norm in Florida, so I had grown accustomed to eating dinner before the sun went down. I was excited to get dressed up and go for a night out on the town. Security called when he arrived at the gate, and a few minutes later my bell rang. When I opened the door, I was pleasantly surprised. Ben was dressed in faded jeans, a long sleeve shirt with the cuffs rolled up, and sandals. This guy didn't look like a typical senior and I thought he was cool the moment that I opened the door.

It was a terrific first date, and we had a lot in common. We ordered the same meal and both had hot fudge sundaes for dessert. Like me, Ben was an avid traveler. We talked the night away, sharing details of prior trips and expressing our desire to do a lot more. Just shy of midnight, we pulled into my building, and I wanted to extend our perfect date by inviting him in for coffee. Before I had a chance to speak, Ben said something snappy that ended our evening. He said, "Give me a call if you're ever in New Jersey." What? Ben said he wasn't looking for a relationship, but was open to something casual. I wasn't sure what casual meant, but whatever it was, I wanted nothing to do with it! Within minutes, my perfect evening with Mr. Cool turned lukewarm. Still reeling over Ben's nerve to tell me to give him a call if I was ever in the area, I thanked him for dinner, shook off my discomfort, and got out of his car. There was no second phone call and no second date.

Six months later, I moved 50 miles upstate to a beautiful new complex with many amenities. It was fun to become involved in some of the different clubs and social activities that were offered. I was casually dating and had gone back to dining before the sun went down. One evening, I got an unexpected phone call. When I picked up, the voice on the other end asked, "Do you remember me? Would you like to go out for a hot fudge sundae?" It was Ben, and he was now living in Florida. I'm not sure why, but I didn't hang up on him. I guess it's because I still thought of him and our pleasant evening together. I'd gone out with other men since then, but there was something about Mr. Cool that intrigued me and I agreed to see him again. We talked for a few minutes, and I told him that I had moved 50 miles north since our last date. I gave the name of my new complex and directions. He didn't say a word, and I thought that we had been disconnected. Then Ben said, "This is crazy, not only do I know the complex you are talking about, but I just moved here!" Within the community itself, there were eight neighborhoods. Ben not only moved to the same complex, but he lived in my exact neighborhood. I hadn't heard from him in six months, and now he could walk to my house!

Our second date turned out to be as great as the first one, and this time he came in for a cup of coffee. I asked him the reason for his quick departure and disappearance six months ago. Ben was honest and straightforward with me. Recently divorced, the last thing he wanted was to be in a committed relation- ship. He wasn't ready to be accountable to someone else again. Ben also thought that I was too fancy for him. This was the first time anybody had referred to me this way, and I found it kind of cute. When I asked him why, he told me that my building was "fancy" with all of the security there. I had to laugh at this. In Florida, there is a gated community on every street corner. I respected Ben's position, but mine was just the opposite. I had been happily married and hoped for that again.

We went out a few more times, and I knew it was time to lay my cards on the table. I explained how important commitment and marriage were to me, and that they were non-negotiable. I also told him that I wasn't willing to invest my time, or myself, in a relationship that had no chance of going anywhere. Ben was leaving to visit his kids later in the week and said he needed time to think about our conversation. I didn't believe anything new would come of it, but I wished him a safe trip and we said goodnight.

Several days later, he called and asked me to please pick him up from the airport. When he got into my car, he was in a delightful mood and said that he had thought a lot about us. I listened. Ben expressed a genuine desire to have a life that was different from the one he had before. While away, he felt blindsided by the feelings that he had for me. He didn't want to lose me and asked me to trust him and give him a chance. Never one for taking risks, especially with a man that expressed little ability to succeed in a committed relationship, my answer even surprised me. I agreed to give things a chance.

It didn't take long for things to take a 180-degree turn and begin to heat up. A monogamous relationship also meant sex. I wasn't nervous per se, but I did worry that I might not measure up to his previous women that had been nothing more than friends with benefits. Petrified that he could have a venereal disease, I told him that I wouldn't sleep with him until he was tested. He passed, and within the year we were married. Not only did I get my happily ever after, but I've learned that it's possible to have more than one soul mate in life. He adores me, my children, and my grandchildren. He is a fabulous cook and is now the only one allowed in our kitchen. I am convinced that it was destiny that brought us together. Ben tells me that he is the lucky one. I tell him that he is right!

Mourning after update: *They continue to travel the globe and have been happily married for over 10 years. Les and Judy have since followed them to Florida.*

MARRIED COUPLES COMMONLY
SOCIALIZE WITH MARRIED FRIENDS.
WHEN ONE OF THOSE COUPLES
BECOMES A SINGLE,
THE DYNAMICS CHANGE.
THE LAST THING THAT ANYONE DESIRES
IS BEING THE SINGLE ONE
AT THE DINNER TABLE OR
AT A SOCIAL EVENT.
TAGGING ALONG SOLO
WITH LONG-TIME FRIENDS
CAN FEEL A BIT UNCOMFORTABLE
AND IS OFTEN TIMES
A LONELY REMINDER OF DAYS GONE BY.

Milk,
Margarine,
and
Men

It had been almost 50 years since my husband, Sal, and I last shared a beach house with my sister Ruthie and our friend Ralph and his family. All of us were filled with the get-up-and-go energy that comes with youth. I remember those trips well. Our three families would pack the cars with suitcases, beach toys, and babies. We'd head to the Jersey shore for a week of glorious, sun-drenched chaos. We spent our days swimming, sunning, and socializing. Although I only had eyes for my wonderful Sal, our friend Ralph was a hunk of a guy with dark, good looks; a George Clooney type by today's standards. Eventually, Ralph and his family moved far away and we lost touch with him and his wife. Over the years, I would sometimes pull out the black-and-white photos that chronicled our modest, yet joyous trips to the beach. Those were the days.

Six months after Sal passed away, I received a star-tling phone call from Ruthie. She asked me if I was sitting down. "What's wrong?" I asked. She laughed, and began to tell me the reason for her call. She had been shopping at the grocery store when she noticed a white-haired man that had a familiarity about him.

There was something about his eyes that caught her attention. Ruthie followed him a few aisles, then on a hunch, she approached him. "Forgive me for staring, but I think I may know you. Are you by chance the Ralph that used to go to the beach with June and me?" Sure enough, it was. After re-introducing herself, they began to reminisce in the canned soup aisle. As I listened to the story, I felt a deep and almost painful sense of nostalgia. For reasons I didn't understand, I also started to feel excited and had a case of butterflies in my stomach.

Ralph explained that he recently lost his wife and had moved back to be closer to family. He was living alone, and ironically was now living only a few miles from where I lived. My sister went on to tell him that Sal had passed away six months earlier. He asked how I was handling the loss, and she told him that I was doing remarkably well. They were recalling some of the fun times we had on our summer trips when Ruthie decided to plant a seed. "I think that June would love to talk to you, to reminisce about old times." He agreed that it would be nice and wrote down his number.

As I listened to the story unfold, my initial delight receded. "You actually told Ralph that I would call him?" I asked in a panic. "I'm not going to call him, and I wish you hadn't put me in this awkward position." Other than my husband, I hadn't been alone with a man in decades, and although my sister assured me that this wouldn't turn into a date, we both knew better. Ruthie was someone who spoke her mind and didn't spend time worrying about the opinions of others. She told me that I was being irrational and to relax. She said he looked great, and it wasn't a big deal. I took his number and hung up the phone.

After the initial shock had subsided, I began to feel curious about seeing Ralph again. I missed my husband, but I also missed having a social life. I went to lunch or an occasional movie with a friend but avoided dinners with couples. I didn't want them paying for me, and they weren't comfortable when I slid money across the table. Although these may seem like trivial matters, it was difficult to strike a comfort level. I often made excuses to my married friends, so that I wouldn't have to join them.

After Sal had been diagnosed with terminal cancer, he fought like hell for a few years. Ruthie knew better than anyone how unbearable Sal's final months were and what a dedicated round-the-clock caretaker I had been. The cancer had physically and mentally destroyed him; eventually morphing him into someone that I no longer knew. Unlike my friends and my family, I had begun my grieving long before his funeral.

Seeing Ralph might actually be fun, I thought, and then I called Ruthie back to thank her for her assertive move. I told her my concern about people seeing me out with a man, and how there would be a lot of whispering and speculating, not to mention criticism. "So what, let them talk." she shot back. I also insisted that my kids might think that I was over the loss of their father, or that I was being insensitive and selfish. My sister voiced her opinion and reminded me that I was the one widowed and spending most nights alone. Ruthie made sense, and I was grateful to have her reassurance. We decided that my kids would survive it if I sought a little companionship and that I was permitted and entitled to have a life of my own.

Calling Ralph was easier than I had anticipated. I waited a couple of days so that I wouldn't appear too anxious, although I had thought of little else in the time leading up to it. He was overjoyed to hear from me and joked that he had been waiting by the phone for my call. His voice had the familiar sound of days gone by, and we talked and laughed easily. He invited me to have lunch with him, and the next day we met at a local restaurant.

He was waiting for me when I arrived. I was in my seventies but still made a nice appearance and had a trim figure. Ralph no longer looked like a movie star, but he wore his age well. During our lunch, he took my hand from across the table and told me how happy he was to see me. He couldn't stop talking about how sweet and beautiful I still was, how much I hadn't changed, and how we seemed to have a lot in common. Although it was a lot to take in, I was enjoying the compliments and all the attention. For the first time in a long time, I was being seen as June the woman, not June the mother and grandmother. He was interested in hearing anything and everything about me, and it felt wonderful to have such a captive audience. After a four-hour lunch, we hugged goodbye, and to my surprise he planted a big wet kiss on my lips. He eagerly set up a dinner date for the upcoming weekend.

I went home and called Ruthie to give my report, telling her that I had enjoyed myself but that I was also feeling some mixed emotions. Although I was charmed and intrigued by him, my sense was that I wasn't going to feel anything more than that. All I knew was that I had enjoyed being in the company of a man and was quite proud of myself for having taken this giant leap. I looked forward to seeing him again but hoped that he wouldn't get ahead of himself. He seemed to be rather forward, but then again, maybe I was just inexperienced at this sort of thing. I told Ruthie that he planted a big wet one on me, and she teased that I must have been irresistible. She showed support for my cautiousness and was ecstatic that I made a second date. She told me to stop overthinking it and have some fun.

Dinner was as pleasant as lunch had been, and Ralph

continued to fawn over me. I didn't share his same gush, but I liked listening to his stories and was just excited to have a male friend. He continued to try to kiss me and even suggested that I sleep over. I didn't feel that sort of chemistry with Ralph and expressed that I was only looking for friendship. When he pulled into my driveway, I thanked him and leaned over to give him a hug. His next action came out of left field; Ralph locked my lips and tried to slip his tongue in my mouth. I'm no prude, but I wasn't prepared for that and jerked away. I said goodnight, then went inside and rinsed my mouth.

I accepted one last dinner invitation in an attempt to steer our friendship down a different path, even though I knew we were probably looking for different things. Maybe it was silly of me to think that we could just be friends, but I enjoyed his company, so it was worth a shot. This time, I told Ralph that I would be picking him up and that dinner would be my treat. During dinner, he grabbed my hands and suggested we have an overnight. I wondered if Ralph had selective memory or if he was just thick. Then, out of nowhere, he leaned across the table and demanded, "Are you going to give me a good kiss tonight"? His childlike outburst was a turn-off, and I just wasn't feeling it. So I leaned across the table and responded with a simple no.

Ralph never did call me again, but that was okay because he was looking for a sexual partner, not just a pal. I wasn't sure yet what the heck I was looking for, but knew that I wasn't going to find it with him. Always the optimist, Ruthie applauded me for my efforts and my courage. Nothing was lost, yet much was gained, and I had stepped out of my comfort zone. I had taken a chance on finding romance again, and had gained a good dose of experience along the way. Most importantly, I will surely do it again.

Mourning after update: *Ruthie still scouts the local grocery stores to find eligible men for her sister. Rumor has it that Ralph is still in search of having someone sleep over.*

PEOPLE WILL SOMETIMES

IMPOSE THEIR OWN EXPECTATIONS

OF HOW WIDOWS

ARE SUPPOSED TO MOURN.

SOME OF THESE PHILOSOPHIES

MAY BEST SOOTHE THE SOULS

OF FRIENDS AND FAMILY,

BUT AT THE SAME TIME

CAN OBSTRUCT NATURAL LONGINGS

FELT BY THE GRIEVER.

I was at Peace. We had Already Said Goodbye

*I try to be an inspiration to other
widows and widowers in my community,
encouraging them to
beat to their own drum and follow their own path.
I understand their inner struggles
and the balancing act that awaits them,
if and when they seek to find love again.*

With eyes still heavy from sleep, I slid my fingers across the sheet to say good morning to him. I felt the vacant spot where he had slept for 30 years, and remembered that he was gone.

Shortly after I graduated from high school, I married Buddy. In those years, you didn't just live with someone, and since we wanted to be together, that meant a wedding. My parents' insisted that I waited until my 18th birthday before walking down the aisle. He was four years older, which seemed like a lot at the time, but we were both just a couple of kids who were madly in love. Our intense love followed us through until the day he died.

Throughout the last 20 years of our marriage, Buddy suffered from an illness that progressively eroded his health and made him feel sick much of the time. There was a period of time when he was physically unable to work for two solid years. We experienced the high that came with news of remission and the low that came with "I'm sorry, there's nothing more we can do." I admired him for how he dealt with his illness, how he helped his children deal with his illness, and how he prepared me for his imminent death. In the final two years, we knew that Buddy was on borrowed time, and he began the tedious process of making sure that I would know what to do when he was gone. It helped me to live with reality, rather than hide behind a smokescreen of denial.

Knowing that we weren't going to be forever helped me to begin saying goodbye early. We talked openly about him dying and, believe it or not, it was a positive part of the process for me. Talking and planning gave us the opportunity to guide one another … preparing both of us for his end and my future. I remember something that he said to me that was noble and generous. "Diane, it's just so unfair to you that I am going to leave you." I couldn't believe his words because he was only 50 years old, and he was about to miss our whole life together. He made me promise that I wouldn't sacrifice myself to a lengthy period of mourning; that I would move forward with my life. He would always say, "Diane, no matter what it takes for you to be happy, just go for it." That was over 25 years ago.

After the funeral, I took one day at a time, not making

any fast decisions in the initial days. I learned that I could get help for anything that I didn't know how to do. I picked myself up and got out of the house early on. I would go to lunch, dinner, and even attend some of the traditional functions that I had gone to with my husband. Finding an escort wasn't an issue because Buddy and I had friends that were widowers. At that time, I felt more comfortable aligning myself with people who had experienced loss because I didn't have to explain what I was feeling. It felt easier to be around people who walked in my shoes, and who didn't ask me the awkward questions for which there weren't any real answers. After Buddy had died, I was uncomfortable going out alone with other couples. This was also when I missed him the most.

I remember the night when a good friend of ours escorted me to a business event, and afterwards he asked me if I wanted to grab a bite. I happily accepted. It was the craziest thing, but I looked across the table at this man that was available and realized that he might be looking at me as a potential girlfriend. I was unable to swallow a bite of food at dinner. It freaked me out, and I had a knee-jerk reaction. I told him that I was uncomfortable and probably wasn't ready for this. My reaction shocked me because I had known this man for years, and this panicky feeling shot out of nowhere. He quickly finished eating while I played with my fork. The minute we stepped outside, I felt I could breathe again, and I relaxed. We actually did go out as friends after that. Knowing that it had been two months since Buddy's death and that I was still in a free-fall, he didn't pressure me to take our friendship to the next level. He was someone that was easy to be with, so I was just enjoying the company.

It was almost four months after my husband died, when a friend called to see if I would be interested in going out with her brother. Through mutual friends I had heard that he was going through a divorce, and I told her he could call me. He did call, and it was sort of funny be-cause he was the one that didn't want to go somewhere local where we might know people. I had already decid-ed that I wouldn't burden myself with others' opinions, but he was worried about public scrutiny. We both were going to be in Chicago at the same time, so we decided to

PENNY BURKE & JOAN PEARLSTEIN DUNN

meet there. Beforehand, I wasn't all that excited about going out with him, and it was more just something nice to do. When he met me downstairs in his lobby, he reached out and put his hand on my shoulder as he said hello. To this day, I can still remember how good that hand felt. We went out to dinner, and the feelings between us were immediate. It's one of those things that can't be explained; it was just an instant connection. It was two heads coming together with a lot of talking, and it just felt good. He was probably the last person that I would have ever seen myself with, because I had never found him all that exciting when Buddy and I would run into him socially. In reality, I think that we are all guilty of prematurely judging people. Had I opted not to go that night, I wouldn't have my wonderful story to share. Our first date turned out to be magic and went on for hours.

I had no fears about following my instincts but always kept an open ear. It's a good idea to hear what others have to say because a person can be so infatuated that they'll overlook things that they need to know. But, at the end of the day, I had been sad for a really long time and I didn't want to feel sad anymore. I was taking a shot at living again, and my husband had left this world with a promise from me that I would make a life for myself. I didn't want to worry if my next-door neighbors, my friends, or even my children thought I was doing the right thing. I knew I was doing the right thing.

In the beginning, I was aware that not everyone would feel the same way about my early departure from mourning. I had a good friend that greeted me in the grocery store, and she started crying when she heard I was dating someone. These were not tears of joy ... she was upset. I knew that this woman didn't have a clue what it felt like to wear my skin, and I also knew that it wasn't my responsibility to educate people on things they couldn't comprehend. I kept looking forward because my husband was gone, and I wasn't going to stay home wringing my hands. I knew that whenever I was smiling, then somewhere out there my Buddy was smiling too.

The new relationship was accelerating quickly, and to put it in perspective I was still writing some last-minute sympathy notes. Shortly after, he asked me to meet him in New York City. Coming home on the plane after our trip, we saw several people that we knew. They impulsively started pouring out their condolences to me, that is, until they saw who was standing next to me. We later laughed about the look on their faces. Clearly, people weren't ready for us to date, but we were ready. Maybe I'm unique, and my approach might have been in the minority. I surely don't think that everyone can move forward as quickly as I did, and I'm not insinuating that I'm stronger than the next woman. I was a young girl when I got married but was a mature woman when my husband died. I truly followed my own code and, with my husband's blessing, I wasn't going to allow anyone to tell me how to conduct myself.

Initially, I relished my new relationship for the wonderful companionship that it offered, but it grew into love. I never allowed myself to compare my new boyfriend to my late husband. If asked, I would always say that the only thing they had in common was they were both males. Nothing else about them was similar, not their personalities, not their backgrounds, not even the dynamics within our relationships. I guess I hadn't been looking for anything in particular, not even a particular quality. I was just open.

We dated for a year and spent a great deal of time together. His well-heeled lifestyle offered luxuries that I wasn't accustomed to and, at times, this took some adjustment on my part. When he was moving into his new home, he asked me to live with him. Although my children were now accepting of him as my boyfriend, I knew that this would infuse a whole new level of discomfort. When I called my daughter to tell her that I was moving in with him, there was silence on the other end of the phone. With a sniffling voice, she said, "So you're putting the final nails into daddy's coffin." I deeply felt for her but was at peace with my decision. I moved in with him, and although we weren't talking marriage, he gave me a ring. Wearing the ring gave me a feeling of belonging, but that feeling was short-lived. We did a lot of entertaining, and it became increasingly uncomfortable to be introduced as his girlfriend. Our wedding took place 23 years ago.

Buddy remains a constant and daily presence in my life. I still think of him when I make decisions about our children or grandkids, and I ask myself, "What would he say?" I still preserve the same love for him now as I did then, but it doesn't have any negative effects on this marriage. I've come to learn that the capacity to love is infinite, and love for one person won't deny it for another.

Mourning after update: *Their marriage continues to evolve, and even after 25 years together, they continue to grow more appreciative of one another. Diane feels so lucky to have had two amazing husbands. She is certain that Buddy is smiling with her.*

OUR LIVES GO ON,

BUT I BELIEVE THAT OUR ABILITY

TO FIND LOVE AGAIN

LIES IN THE CHOICES THAT WE MAKE.

FOR ME IT MEANT

EXPLORING THE NEW WORLD

OF INTERNET DATING.

FOR YOU IT MAY MEAN GOING TO

YOUR HIGH SCHOOL REUNION OR

CALLING AN OLD BOYFRIEND

THAT YOU HEARD IS NOW

SINGLE OR WIDOWED.

THE IMPORTANT THING IS

TO BE PROACTIVE AND

TO JUST DO IT!

From Granny Panties to Thongs: Vol 2

Your Story Here

When you're ready, we'd love to hear from you
Please visit us at
grannypantiestothongs.com

CPSIA information can be obtained at www.ICGtesting.com
Printed in the USA
LVOW06s1708090314

376633LV00024B/733/P